new **organic** architecture
The **breaking** wave

new **organic**
architecture

The **breaking** wave

David **Pearson**

UNIVERSITY OF CALIFORNIA PRESS
Berkeley and Los Angeles

University of California Press

Berkeley and Los Angeles

Published by arrangement with Gaia Books Limited

Library of Congress Cataloging-in-Publication Data

Pearson, David, 1940
    New organic architecture : the breaking wave / David Pearson.
       p. cm.
    Includes bibliographical references and index.
    ISBN 0-520-23288-7 (alk. paper) -- ISBN 0-520-23289-5 (pbk : alk. paper)
     1. Organic architecture. 2. Nature (Aesthetics) I. Title

NA682.O73 P43 2001
720'.47--dc21
                                 2001027442

Printed and bound by Oriental Press, Dubai, UAE

10 9 8 7 6 5 4 3 2 1

previous page: The central dome of the Catholic
church at Szàzhalombàtta, Imre Makovecz.

facing page: Earth filled "superadobe" tubes at Cal-
Earth, California, developed by Nader Khalili.

contents

Watts Towers, Los Angeles, USA.

Detail of Ionic volute, Ephesus, Turkey.

Price residence, Corona del Mar,
California, USA, Bart Prince.

part 2

80 Living organic architecture

Introduction

Organic architecture is a living tradition that is taking on new and exciting directions. It is not a unified movement but is diverse, perverse, contradictory, and mercurial. Always controversial and difficult to pin down, it is best experienced "in the round" with all one's senses by visiting real buildings. Sometimes called "the other tradition", it has a long and celebrated history, from Ancient Greece to Art Nouveau. Organic architecture is rooted in a passion for life, nature, and natural forms, and is full of the vitality of the natural world with its biological forms and processes. Emphasizing beauty and harmony, its free-flowing curves and expressive forms are sympathetic to the human body, mind, and spirit. In a well-designed "organic" building, we feel better and freer.

The fact that the rectilinear, orthogonal mode came to dominate the 20th century is a reflection of materialist values of an industrially driven age. The post-industrial age is awakening to a new world, which also echoes an older and wiser vision. The re-emergence of organic design, represents a new freedom of thought; an expression of hope for the future. This is affecting most fields of design from products and furniture, lighting and textile design to architecture, landscape architecture, and interior design. As this occurs, organic design is becoming less a fringe style than a mainstream design trend.

The new "free style" approach has also been influenced by modern philosophy as expounded by such writers as Fritjof Capra, and scientific ideas as diverse as advanced astrophysics, chaos theory, and James Lovelock's Gaia theory (that describes the living Earth, "Gaia", as a self-regulating super organism). There is a parallel here with the effect that Charles Darwin's revolutionary theory of evolution had on Victorian architecture, inspiring decorative natural forms and motifs. Modern information technology and the rapid spread of computer-aided design (CAD) to all fields of architecture and design, has helped to free up design and designers' creative processes. With the latest three-dimensional design software it is much easier to design and model sophisticated and complex shapes and forms. No longer need the straight line, right angle, and cube be the dominant

Thames Riverlife – a sustainable organic scheme by the author in association with David Newman for a major exhibit in London celebrating the River Thames and its riverlife habitats from source to sea. An impressive 30-metre (100-ft) grass and sedum-covered dome and circular walkway houses indoor aquaria and outdoor ponds representing source spring, upper and lower rivers, estuary, and sea. It is not only a pleasure to experience organic buildings, it is a delight to design them – as it has been for the author who has worked with the Wildfowl & Wetlands Trust on organic exhibition buildings at The Wetland Centre, London. Over 400 hectares (100 acres) of ponds, lagoons, and marshes have been created where imaginative exhibits represent both global wetlands and British waterlife.

features. Using the "strength through shape principle", curved forms such as arches, vaults, domes, and spheres are stronger, more efficient, and more economical than the equivalent rectilinear structures. Both modern and traditional materials can be used organically: new lightweight, tensile tent structures emulate the idea of the Native American Indian tepee, while modern curving earth or strawbale-built walls and vaults rediscover an ancient vernacular.

Organic thinking can also be seen as part of the expression of the feminization of society (or re-balancing the feminine in Western society). This approach is not new. It is a very old tradition stretching back to times when feminine values were more prevalent. This way of thinking can be traced back to Earth Mother goddess cults and can be seen in the beautiful and flowing art and artefacts of the Anatolian, Minoan, Etruscan, and Ancient Greek cultures. There is a correlation too between straight line and rectangle, and angular, masculine design and mechanistic politics.

Organic architecture is not a nostalgic style. It will always fascinate and inspire, and is being reincarnated today as a new international movement that combines a respect for nature with a celebration of the beauty and harmony of natural forms, flows, and systems. In the new millennium a more holistic and organic image of the universe is emerging, and demanding new forms of expression that reflect the variety and creativity of nature itself. Like a breaking wave, this new and exciting paradigm is sweeping over the world and transforming architecture and design for the 21st century.

Inspired by the non-linearity and creative forces of nature and biological organisms, organic architecture is visually poetic, radical, idiosyncratic and environmentally aware; it embodies harmony of place, person and materials. Organic architecture is multi-faceted, free and surprising. Yet its myriad images, ever changeable and overlapping, all grow and flower form the same seed – the inspiration of nature.

Eight key themes drawn from the words and work of organic architects new and old are illustrated in the introductory pages: "building as nature", "continuous present", "form follows flow", "of the people", "of the hill", "of the materials", "youthful and unexpected", and "living music". The main part of the book is in two parts. After a brief introductory photo-essay, Part One gives a thematic overview of organic architecture: its roots and concepts, its sources of inspiration from natural forms, fascination with geometry, and the environmental challenges it presents. Part Two is a unique review of the work of architects drawn from 15 countries, whose work reflects these concerns. The 30 profiled architects write about their own approaches in their own words.

Pond Zone building inspired by a Neolithic roundhouse. Designed by the author to house a dramatic "pond-scape" exhibit, this eight-metre (21-ft) high conical thatched pavilion is built of vernacular materials, including tree trunk, strawbale, and lime plaster walls.

building as nature

"Organic architecture strives to connect the parts of the building which are nearest to the earth – the foundations of the walls in particular – closely to the earth. It also strives to construct them from materials which have been extracted from the earth itself. The upper structures should be light, as if heaven were descending upon the earth." **Imre Makovecz**

"Above all, organic architecture should constantly remind us not to take Mother Nature for granted – work with her and allow her to guide your life. Inhibit her, and humanity will be the loser."
Kendrick Bangs Kellogg

"…a truer understanding of how we see, with our mind and eye, is the foundation of everything organic. Man's eye and brain evolved over aeons of time, most of which were within the vast untrammelled and unpaved landscape of our Edenic biosphere! We must go to Nature for our models now, that is clear!"
Daniel Liebermann

"Our decisions about building must come out of our consciousness of the planet if we do not want to be incriminated in its death. We must look to the wellbeing of the Earth itself and all who live here."
Eric Furnémont

Nature is the fundamental and recurring inspiration of organic architecture. Living organisms, both in their outward forms and in their inner structures, offer endless ideas and concepts for design. Organic architecture works with metamorphosis (the process of growth and change), and the notion of "design from within", whereby each design starts from a seed concept and grows outward, changing in form. More than this, a building is seen as an organism, an indivisible whole, and humans are seen as part of nature, not above her. Ecological concerns have increasingly become the focus and, as today's science reveals more of the extraordinary and wonderful structure of nature, designers can draw on a limitless source of new ideas.

Lutheran Church, Siófok, Hungary, by Imre Makovecz.

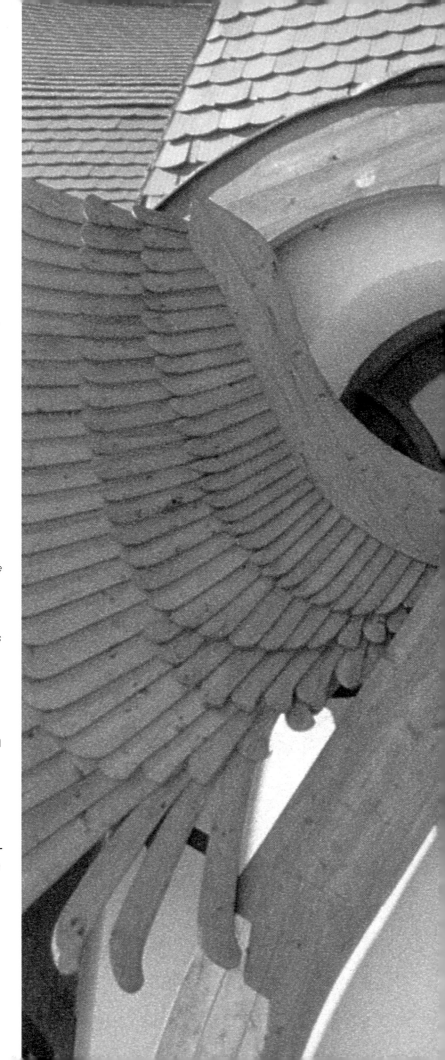

continuous present

"Everything is the same except composition and as the composition is different and always going to be different everything is not the same. So then I as a contemporary creating the composition in the beginning was groping toward a continuous present, a using everything, a beginning again and again." **Bruce Goff**

"Our lives and architecture fuse as a continual metamorphosis of being and becoming: a journey of destruction and creation – a joyful dance between polarities and paradoxes; a way of transformation and under-standing." **Gregory Burgess**

A special characteristic of organic design is that it is a continuous process, never finished, always in a state of change. For Bruce Goff it meant "beginning again and again", existing rather like an old Zen master, in a state of the "continuous present". This brings originality and freshness to a design that never repeats itself. Antoní Gaudí and César Manrique both preferred to develop their designs on the day, at the site, working with the craftspeople rather than fixing ideas entirely as drawings on paper. Gaudí's enormously ambitious Sagrada Familia continues to be built today in this spirit, as a tribute to this continuous "way" or Tao of design.

Pavilion of Japanese Art, Los Angeles County Museum of Art, USA. Designed by Bruce Goff and completed after his death by Bart Prince.

form follows flow

"For America today organic architecture interprets (will eventually build) this local embodiment of human freedom. This natural architecture seeks spaciousness, grace and openness; lightness and strength so completely balanced and logical that it is a new integrity…" **Frank Lloyd Wright**

"But I do know as a designer that when we approach the design of buildings and places by working with dynamic flows as well as static forms; when we think of the building as an organism as well as an object; when our clients become true partners rather than masters or victims, then we have a possibility of building an ecological present that increases our children's chances to create a liveable future." **Sim Van der Ryn**

The form of a building should follow the flow of energy, and be created by it. Architecture needs to flow with, not against, the dynamic forces of nature. This applies to all forms of energy: structural forces, wind, heat and water currents, earth energies, electrical and magnetic fields, as well as the subtle human energies of body, mind, and spirit. The flows of natural forces are curvilinear and cyclic and organic forms of architecture therefore naturally arise out of the dictum "form follows flow".

right: The Solomon R. Guggenheim Museum, New York, USA, Frank Lloyd Wright.

inset: Water flow forms by John Wilkes at the ING Bank, Amsterdam, the Netherlands.

of the people

"Buildings are meant for people – and this includes literate, illiterate, young and old...Each individual, each community has its own preferences. Hence they should be allowed to express themselves symbolically. ...Form should not be finite but should be amorphous so that the experience within is loose, meandering and multiple."
Balkrishna Doshi

"We want to attain spaces adaptable to the human body, like the womb or an animal's lair. Like the troglodytes who carved a niche for themselves out of the earth, or igloo builders, this is not a regression to primitive ways but a premeditated reconciliation."
Javier Senosiain

"...community participation and the use of local materials were the basic conditions. We looked for an interaction with nature through layering intuitively conceived forms and natural forms in the environment...The result was a feeling of joint ownership and collaborative effort that none of those involved had imagined." **Shoei Yoh**

Organic design places special emphasis on developing a sensitive and creative relationship with both the client and the users of the building. Designing from the "inside out" means that, instead of having preconceived ideas about form and structure, design begins with the community and the people and expresses their needs and wishes, even their personal idiosyncrasies. Designing for comfort is important, too. Canadian architect Douglas Cardinal talks of "wrapping" the shape and form of each space around the function. Curvilinear interiors and fittings are natural outcomes. Some architects feel that, for a project to be a truly organic whole, everything must be considered including the furniture and interior decoration.

Hussain-Doshi Gufa, Ahmedabad, India by Balkrishna Doshi.

of the hill

"Fortune has seen fit to make our abode. I hope that my work may be instructive, showing my respect for every part of the earth, with its own materials and traditions, while adding only the best part of progress, without breaking the harmony of the place." **César Manrique**

"The form...came about due to my understanding of the nature of the site and grew from it as a plant might, in the sense that it belongs there and wouldn't have come into being in this form in any other location." **Bart Prince**

It was Frank Lloyd Wright who said that the relation of a building to its site is better expressed as "of the hill" rather than "on the hill". Ideally, an organic building will seem to grow out of its site and be unique to that site. The challenges of awkward sites and unusual locations actually help organic architects to arrive at imaginative and unexpected solutions. Urban sites are especially challenging to organic ideas as the built context is often orthogonal and conventional. But it is better to build on urban or reused land rather than virgin land. Today, a prime concern for organic architects on any site is the reduction of human impact on the environment and wildlife habitats.

Mirador del Río, Lanzarote, Canary Islands, by César Manrique.

of the materials

"My dreams were of a simple house, built with human hands out of simple materials of this world: the elements – Earth, Water, Air, and Fire. To build a house out of earth, then fire and bake it in place, fuse it like a giant hollow rock. The house becoming a kiln, or a kiln becoming a house. Then to glaze this house with fire to the beauty of a ceramic glazed vessel." **Nader Khalili**

"To create an architecture of meaning and beauty we need to return to the source – nature. We should make use of materials and innovation provided by the natural world and put them to good use according to their true nature, not merely to imitate the appearances of the past…But if we…use nature as a basis of design we can create a new, evoloutionary architecture."
Eugene Tsui

Organic forms spring from the qualities of the building materials chosen. The properties of the material dictate the ideal and optimum form and shape of the structure. Traditional materials – earth, straw, wood – are celebrated in organic building and now, new materials offer fresh opportunities for structural innovation and surprise. Organic architects have always embraced new materials and sometimes like to use unusual materials in unusual places. But today, materials need also to be healthy, ecologically sound, and resource efficient. Most of all, organic architecture allows the materials to express themselves and draws its spirit from their inner qualities.

Brick dome, Cal-Earth, Hesperia,
California, by Nader Khalili.

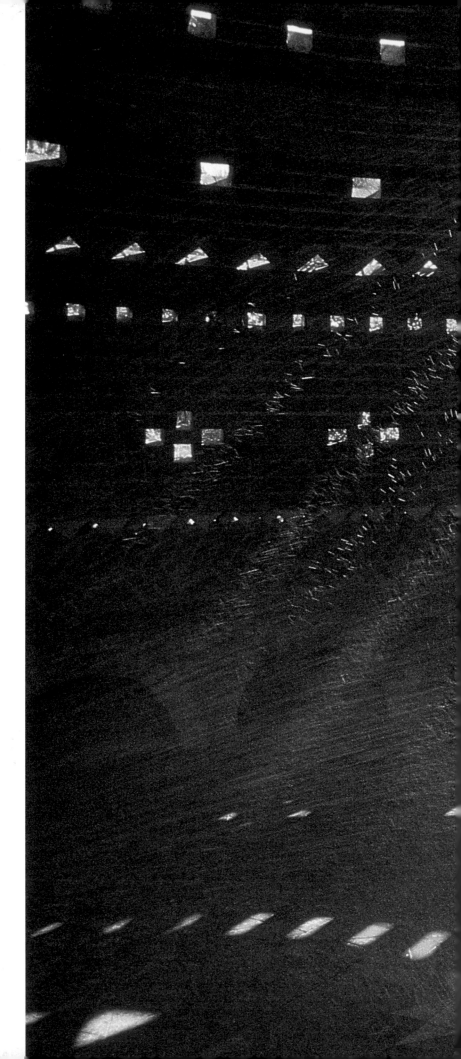

youthful and unexpected

"Designing is a journey in a way. You set off to find out, to learn. You accept the unexpected. Each project is a new start, and you are in unexplored territory. You are a Robinson Crusoe of modern times." **Renzo Piano**

"I retain, paradoxically, delight in the fire of action, of creation, in the very instant. This delight keeps one young." **Jacques Gillet**

"The environment is something to be played with as well as in. Interactive rather than passive, it also plays with you, eliciting a reaction from you as you move through it, while also sculpting your movement…As in the imagination of a child, everything can be, and is, alive." **Koval**

Organic architects are often very individual characters. Some like to be maverick, provocative, and even anti-establishment. Their architecture feels youthful and playful with a childlike love of fun. Their designs, being sometimes purposely eccentric, are surprising and unexpected. Buildings can also be powerful or disturbing in their symbolism, mythology, and use of metaphors from Mackovecz's dark forests of tree-like forms and flashing angels' wings to the cryptic masonic and Catalonian allusions in Gaudí's Güell Park or Senosiain's sensual womb-like spaces.

Tjibaou Cultural Village, Nouméa, New Caledonia, by Renzo Piano.

living music

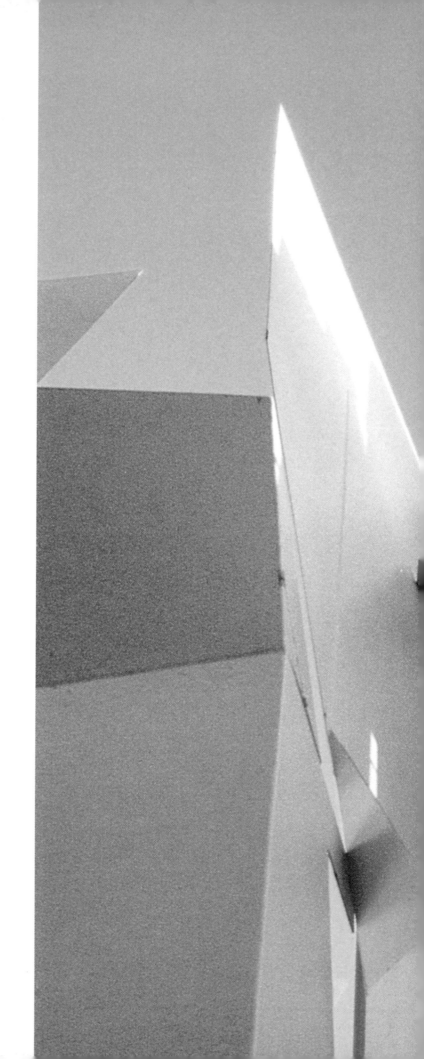

"The building site as it expands
is like a quartet in four movements.
The sub-foundation is a powerful allegro moderato.
The lofty terrace is the adagio cantabile,
huge movement both quiet and steady.
The whole orchestration is to come.
Capitals, vaults, frames and stained-glass constitute
the scherzo,
moving from sostenuto to prestissimo.
The superstructure is the rondo finale apassionnato."
Jacques Gillet

Organic architecture is living, rather than frozen, music, performed in the continuous present. With its juxtaposition of harmonies and discords, its diverse rhythms and syncopated movement, and its asymmetrical proportions and structure, it has closer affinities with modern music than with classical compositions. Organic is always modern and futuristic, drawing on new science and mathematics and seeing Nature herself as modern and ever new. Even the numerical laws of chaos theory and fractals can generate the music and patterns of organic architecture and design.

The Experimental Permanent Building
Site of Sculpture-Architecture (PEBSA) at
Ouffet, Belgium, by Jacques Gillet.

part **1**

sources and inspirations

Roof of traditional Shona hut,
Great Zimbabwe.

"For some, organic is curved, organic is asymmetrical, organic is natural materials, organic is individualistic, organic is holistic."

Sidney K. Robinson, "The Continuous Present of Organic Architecture",
Architectural Design 7/8, 1993

"Organic creation in art and architecture is not a style but a principle. No single style could possibly encompass the organic principle. It is a limitless paradigm."

Eli Bornstein, "Notes on the Mechanical and the Organic in Art and Nature", *The Structuralist 35/36*, 1995-96

"Organic form is a space-time structure. It creates its space-time. Being in an organic form we partake of its distinctive space-time; its possibility of non-local interconnections over multiple dimensions."

Mae-Wan Ho, "New Age of Organicism", *Architectural Design Profile* 129 "New Science = New Architecture", 1997

"New directions that dismiss organic creation as some past or dead style in an attempt to invent something entirely "new" miss its underlying reality as a universal creative principle."

Eli Bornstein, "Notes on the Mechanical and the Organic in Art and Nature", *The Structuralist 35/36*, 1995-96

"Perhaps a new organicism, stripped of inhibitions and guilt complexes, and not regimented into a tendency, but free to expand in directions congenial to the Earth's different places, might be an architectural outcome of the lesson of this moment."

Editorial, *Domus* special issue "La nuove organicita", March 1996

"Virtually all those who referred to 'organic architecture' (including classicists, such as Vitruvius and Alberti, and Modernists, such as Gropius and Wright) insisted on work that shows fractal self-similarity. 'Unity with variety'."

Charles Jencks, *The Architecture of the Jumping Universe*, 1995

"But Organic Architecture does not end with prima donnas. It is really 'the other tradition' something often submerged, which is not published by many commercial magazines, because it is felt to be out of fashion. Perhaps, one day or another... Organic Architecture will come into the open."

Bruno Zevi, "Organic in Italy", *Architectural Review*, June 1985

"Whereas elsewhere the dynamics of geometry are merely presented in repetition so that like balances like, here one is concerned with the growth of one out of the other."
Rudolf Steiner, 1922

"I bring you a new Declaration of Independence...An Organic Architecture means more or less an organic society. Organic ideals of integral building reject rules imposed by exterior aestheticism or mere taste, and so would the people to whom such architecture would belong reject external impositions upon life as were not in accord with the nature and character of the man who had found his work and the place where he could be happy and useful because of it... beauty seems to have made no sense for long at any time. I believe that time has come when beauty must make sense for our time at least... In this modern era Art, Science, Religion – these three will unite and be one, unity achieved with organic architecture as centre."
Frank Lloyd Wright, address to the Royal Institute of British Architects, 1939

Real architecture arrives as "a concept which grows from within outward through the natural use of materials – directed and ordered by the creative spirit – so that the form is one with function."

Bruce Goff, 1942

"In order to create for life, we must create as nature does, organically and not geometrically."
Hugo Håring, "Approach to Form", 1925-6

"All perfectly beautiful forms must be composed of curves; since there is hardly any common natural form in which it is possible to discover a straight line."

John Ruskin, *The Seven Lamps of Architecture*, 1880

"...we, in our art, are to follow Nature's processes, Nature's rhythms, because those processes, those rhythms are vital, organic, coherent, logical above all book-logic, and flow uninterrupted from cause to effect."
Louis Sullivan, "Kindergarten Chats", 1918

"Architecture is organic when the spatial arrangement of room, house and city is planned for human happiness, material, psychological and spiritual. The organic is based therefore on a social idea and not on a figurative idea. We can only call architecture organic when it aims at being human before it is humanist."
Bruno Zevi, "Towards an Organic Architecture", 1945

Roots and concepts

Primitive vernacular architecture was innately organic, based on natural forms and structures and simple, local materials. More deeply, it was part of a spiritual continuum of survival and fertility, life and death that linked earth to spirit. Egyptian and Ancient Greek civilizations studied natural forms and the human body and abstracted them as geometry. They used the circle, ellipse, triangle, and rectangle to derive harmonious proportions for their shrines and temples and so promote harmony between themselves and their elemental gods and spirits of Earth and cosmos. Fundamental discoveries included geometric relationships such as the Golden Section (see page 65), generator of the logarithmic spiral, a basic curve of life and growth.

The ascendancy of geometry

Plato believed that all things flow and change in nature but are directed by eternal and immutable patterns, forms, or ideas that are the true reality. Aristotle, however, as a founder of the scientific approach, used observation to understand and classify nature. In architectural terms both contributed to key ideas and concepts that run through organic design and the debate between holistic and analytical approaches that has continued ever since.

The Roman, Vitruvius, agreed with his forebears that the human body, with its modular construction, is the ideal expression of nature's unity. His *homo quadratus* – the figure of a man, with extended arms and feet, fits neatly into what were considered the most perfect geometrical figures – the square and circle. The Romans moved on from philosophy to practice and to develop arches, vaults, and domes – structurally stronger and more economical of materials than earlier straight post and beam designs.

Toward the end of the Roman Empire theories of proportion lost their original divine significance and became a series of secular rules applied by rote to any building of importance. Later, in the Byzantine Empire, Christian spirituality re-inspired architecture with ideas of divine proportion and the mystique

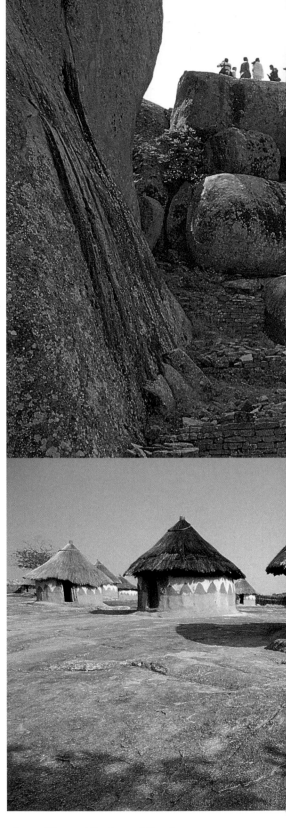

above: The architecture of Great Zimbabwe is rooted in the land. Its walls flow over the landscape in a harmony of curves, echoing the natural forms of boulder and hill. Within stone wall compounds stand the traditional round dhaka and pole huts of the Shona people.

right: The soft tufa rock of Cappadocia, Turkey, has been the home of troglodyte dwellers since prehistoric times.

of numbers, and developed the Roman form of the dome placed on a square to create the typical Byzantine cross-in-square church plan.

Divine geometry was also very much alive in the Islamic world. Here representation of the human and other animal forms was strictly prohibited. Mathematics and abstract geometry were the only appropriate expression of order and perfection created by Allah. Thus pure geometric shapes – circle, square, polygon, and star – were employed to produce the timeless Islamic architectural language of cupola, half dome, tunnel vault, horseshoe arch, stalactite "pendentive", and rich ornamentation. Like Allah, the limitless one, building forms, spaces, and ornament seem to cascade, like fractals, into the distance without end.

Early Celtic art, like nature, abhorred straight lines and preferred the organic forms of the tree, plants, water, and earth. Rather than representing nature as it appears, the Celtic artist expressed a mystical and ambiguous world of highly stylized abstract forms. The motifs ranged from geometric patterns to chevrons, circles, whorls, tendrils, spirals, and, later, animals. Used as repeating and entwined patterns, they were executed with free-flowing grace and beauty and also a sense of wit and individuality.

Gothic architecture absorbed elements of both Greek geometry and pagan Celtic expression. Master masons revitalized the sacred purpose of proportion and used plant forms for decoration. The circle was the basic controlling device for Gothic cathedral design. The whole structure derived from underlying star diagrams, subdivided by polygons (especially, pentagons and decagons, which relate directly to the Golden Section), generated harmonious and "heavenly" proportions. The pointed Gothic arch and vault, being more akin to the parabolic arch, shed structural loads more efficiently than the massive Roman semicircular arch. This innovation allowed unrivalled building heights to be reached with an apparent lightness and delicacy never before imagined possible in stone – a real flowering of the organic in architecture!

Renaissance and rationalism

With the Renaissance came renewed interest in Classical theories of proportion based on human form. Michelangelo held that knowledge of the human figure was vital to a comprehension of architecture. Alberti remarked that a building must appear whole like an organism and Leonardo da Vinci made his famous drawing of Vitruvius's *homo quadratus*. But the Renaissance also brought new science. When Descartes stated "I have described the earth, and

Detail of Ionic volute, Ephesus, Turkey.

all the visible world, as if it were a machine" he heralded the Age of Reason and gave birth to modern scientific method. With this new age came a conviction that architecture was a science, too, and that each part of a building, inside and out, had to be integrated into one system of mathematical ratios. The opposing visions of holism and mechanistic science began to diverge into separate camps.

For the people and by the people

As a reaction to the dominance of this overly scientific view sprang the desire of the Gothic Revival for freedom from Classical rules and a return to what were seen as truer spiritual and holistic values. New architectural principles proposed by Ruskin, Pugin, and Viollet-le-Duc drew inspiration from the forms and processes of nature and promoted medieval building traditions such as hierarchy of functions and forms, structural expression, truth to materials, craft skills, and rich polychromy and ornament. The Oxford University Museum, by Deane and Woodward, and the Natural History Museum, London, by Waterhouse, are examples of these principles in action.

"Art for the people and by the people" was the cry of William Morris, one of the founders of the Arts and Crafts Movement. And it was these social aims (reiterated later by Frank Lloyd Wright) that underpinned the movement's concentration on creativity, naturalness, craft production, and co-operative effort to counter the spread of machine production and poor quality mass-produced goods. Red House, Bexley Heath, Kent, by Philip Webb, echoes the medieval but is highly original in its internal layout. Its asymmetrical massing and creative use of materials embodying, as Morris wished, the concept that a building should be like an organic being.

The rejection of 19th century stylistic imitations for a simpler, more abstract approach with natural continuous forms paved the way for the wilder fantasies of Art Nouveau. Exotic sources, such as those from Islam, Japan, and the Far East, and folk art were used in novel ways to create this shimmering new modern style. Its influence quickly spread throughout Europe, from Munich's Jugendstil (youth style) to Barcelona's Modernistas, and on to the USA. But it was the deep, and sometimes near pantheistic or mystical, affinity with the natural world that was the universal source of inspiration. Typical was the use of long, curved, asymmetrical lines somewhat reminiscent of Celtic art. Inspired by the delicacy of such living forms as sinuous vine tendrils, flower stems, buds, and insect wings, the line could be gentle and

Sinuous curves and membrane-like windows of the Hotel Tassel, Brussels, by Victor Horta.

graceful or powerful and tense like a whiplash. In architecture, ornament and structure became fused into a free-flowing, plastic, organic unity. Structures resembled sinuous vegetative growths, windows appeared as diaphanous membranes, and materials an exotic palette of brick, stone, mosaic, terracotta, wrought and cast iron, stained glass, and wood veneers. Victor Horta's revolutionary Hotel Tassel, Brussels, exemplified this style as did the light and elegant Glasgow School of Art by Charles Rennie Mackintosh. So too did the robust and curvilinear furniture and interiors of Horta's compatriot Henry van de Velde. The latter, however, later rejected ornament and what he saw as sentimental and degenerate romanticism of Art Nouveau for a clean, logical and rationalist style that embraced the machine. With the re-appearance of the dominant straight line and right angle, van de Velde's cool and restrained Art School, Weimar, and Werkbund Theatre, Cologne, ushered in the Bauhaus, the International Style, and the predominant course of mainstream modern architecture. But before this took hold, Expressionism had a brief but influential life with such renowned buildings as the Einstein Tower, Potsdam, by Erich Mendelsohn. Intended as a vision of new monolithic concrete architecture, he aimed to create streamlined exteriors and organically flowing interiors that defied traditional structural laws.

Metaphor and materials

For Antoni Gaudí, supreme and passionate master of the organic, the straight line belonged to men and the curved line to God. Always at the bizarre and surrealist end of the organic spectrum, the early medieval, Islamic, and Catalan influences gave way, in his later work such as Casa Batlló and Casa Milà (La Pedrera – the quarry), to extreme plasticity that superbly integrates structure, materials, and sculptural form. Gaudí closely observed natural forms and was a bold innovator of advanced structural systems. He designed "equilibrated" structures (that stand like a tree, needing no internal bracing or external buttressing) with catenary, hyperbolic, and parabolic arches and vaults, and inclined columns and helicoidal (spiral cone) piers, first cleverly predicting complex structural forces via string models hung with weights (his results now confirmed by computer analysis). He loved to instil his projects with many levels of meaning and delighted in metaphor and symbol, overtly religious as in the church of the Sagrada Familia but more subtle and mysterious as in Güell Park with its strange mix of Catalan and masonic symbolism. Yet, its weird pinnacled lodges, serpentine mosaic bench, and winding rustic viaducts all evoke the exuberance of youth.

Güell Park, Barcelona by Antoni Gaudí is an imaginative city-garden project with its winding shady paths, Doric-style "market", and great terrace with its famous snake-like *trencadís* (broken tile) mosaic bench. It is entered via two pavilions, one of which (below) has a roof shaped like an elephant howdah and crowned with a mosaic fly agaric mushroom.

Casa Milà (La Pedrera), Barcelona by Gaudí is an UNESCO World Heritage Site. The sheer audacity of its rippling and flowing façade, its shimmering mosaic and tortuous metal balconies, all reminiscent of foaming waves and storm-tossed sea, are truly breathtaking, even today. The undulating roof terrace, resting on a group of parabolic brick arches (see also page 66), is surmounted by surreal chimneys with mask-like tops.

Alvar Aalto brought a Scandinavian clarity, simplicity, and lightness to organic design. He was a genius at handling asymmetrical massing of diverse volumes and gradually moved from earlier angular forms (Town Hall, Säynatsälo) to evolve vigorous curved forms (Finlandia Concert Hall, Helsinki). He could create a fluidity of space and quality of natural lighting and colour that were poetical, and use simple natural materials, particularly wood, in new and creative ways so as to "allow the materials to express themselves". Jørn Utzon, the Danish architect who worked briefly in Aalto's office, evolved his own original style based on nature, and ultimately won the design competition for the Sydney Opera House with its billowing white concrete "sails".

From inner purpose to outward appearance

But it was in the USA that organic architecture began its great modern flowering. "By speaking generally, outward appearances resemble inner purposes" was one way Louis Sullivan described his famous axiom that form follows function – a key concept for organic design. Influenced by the massive Romanesque style of H.H. Richardson's Marshall Field Warehouse, Chicago, he evolved his own monumental round-arched style first used in the Auditorium Building, Chicago, and his unique feathery and vegetal Art Nouveau ornament. At first, he used this sparingly to adorn specific parts of his otherwise plain functional steel-frame offices but later, his mature work attempted to fuse function and ornament into a unified whole.

Perhaps it was the Celt in him from his Welsh mother that gave Frank Lloyd Wright a special love of nature. It was certainly reinforced via early readings of Ruskin and Viollet-le-Duc and working with his mentor Sullivan. He wished his buildings to be part of nature and would often choose sites close to woods, rock formations, or even waterfalls as with Fallingwater, Pennsylvania. Like "a thing growing out of the nature of the thing", the concept of the building would emerge naturally out of the site. If nature was absent, he would provide ample space for plantings in and around the building or turn the building inward and fill the centre with trees and plants. He disliked static symmetry and preferred the dynamic irregularities of nature and of Gothic architecture, where according to Ruskin a plan might "shrink into a turret, expand into a hall, coil into a staircase, or

facing page: The large spiral tower of the Solomon R. Guggenheim Museum, New York, by Frank Lloyd Wright, specially illuminated for an installation by Nam June Paik.

below: Wright's design for Taliesin West, Scottsdale, Arizona superbly integrates the building with the natural desert landscape.

right: Herb Greene's
Prairie House, Norman,
Oklahoma, 1961.

spring into a spire". He developed geometrical themes beyond the rectangle and experimented with circles and spirals divided into 30 and 60 degree angles such as the Jacobs House, Wisconsin, an innovative solar hemicycle, and culminating in the dramatic springing coil of the Guggenheim Museum, New York. Linked to his earlier desire to produce low-cost homes and communities, which he termed "Usonian", he called for a universal organic society via his new "Declaration of Independence" (see page 29).

The organic legacy

Frank Lloyd Wright is, for many, the true father of organic architecture. He was not only an architect of rare genius, he was a charismatic speaker, writer, and educator, who inspired a generation of young architects who have continued to work and innovate in the same spirit of design. These include Paolo Soleri, Arthur Dyson (page 206), Dan Liebermann (page 122), Kendrick Bangs Kellogg (page 196), and John Watson (page 172).

Advised by Sullivan and Wright to avoid college if he wished to keep his individual creativity, Bruce Goff was largely self taught from diverse sources in art, architecture, and music (see page 154). A maverick, he believed that designing a building was an act of self-discovery and that one's own personal development, and that of the client and students, were more important than adhering to any style or movement. He worked in what he called the "continuous present", his maxim being "beginning again and again". Goff described his approach "as a concept that grows from within outward". He liked to play with competing natural elements, earth, air, fire, and water, and delighted in combining opposites – heavy masonry with light walls and roofs, free-flowing space with angular geometric forms, solid structure with crystalline or lacy elements, and natural materials with prefabricated parts.

This futuristic organic architecture superbly integrates many complex elements The Bavinger House, Oklahoma, is a continuous logarithmic spiral of open-space platforms, suspended by cables from a central mast. The spaces seem to defy gravity and float over one another and the indoor pools below, yet are rooted in the ground via the massive stone core. A natural teacher, he wanted to establish a school of art and architecture called "Kebyar" – a Balinese word for the process of flowering. Although he never did so, he influenced many young architects such as Herb Greene, Bart Prince (see page 86), Mickey Muennig (see page 152), and Eugene Tsui (see page 182), some of whom formed Friends of Kebyar, the US association of organic architects.

above: Bruce Goff's Bavinger House, Norman, Oklahoma, 1950. In 1987 the American Institute of Architects panel wrote of the Bavinger House,
"It spirals joyously into the Oklahoma sky, cut loose from the earth by a mind as free as the prairie landscape, a celebration of the spirit of man and nature united in architecture."

From seed to plant

A separate strand of the organic tradition has its roots in the Germanic cultural tradition. Rudolf Steiner, the Austrian thinker, was so impressed with the studies of Johann Wolfgang von Goethe into morphology and the metamorphosis of plants and animals that he referred to Goethe as "the Galileo of the organic". This, together with Goethe's theory of colour, had a deep impact on Steiner's later life and his anthroposophic architectural theories. Steiner developed a special intuitive process he termed *organischen Baugedanken* (organic structural thoughts) to help comprehend the essence of an organic being. He never imitated natural forms, nor were his designs allegories or symbols for anything but themselves. "Man can only experience true harmony of soul where what his soul knows to be its most valuable thoughts, feelings and impulses are mirrored for his senses in the forms, colours and, so on, of his surroundings." From this projection of bodily feelings into building forms, known as *Einfühlung*, it follows that well-designed buildings can exert a healing and spiritually supportive effect on both individuals and society. His two Goetheanums were a dramatic illustration of this new style of architecture that united spirit and matter with a living interaction between part and whole, the crucial link being the metamorphosis between the small (seed) and the large (plant) whereby the new form is always, as in nature, prefigured in the previous form. In his later work he evolved related concepts

below: Christopher Day sensitively combines the anthroposophic principles of Rudolf Steiner with vernacular materials and traditions in his design for a retreat in Wales.

facing page: The first Goetheanum in Dornach, Switzerland, 1913 (it was destroyed by fire 1922), was a dramatic illustration of Rudolf Steiner's attempt at a new style of architecture that was both organic and functional. The form-making principles of the natural world were applied to create an organism-like relation between part and whole, while the principle of metamorphosis in both small detail and larger plan related to Goethe's studies of biological morphology.

above: La Frégate Café, St Helier, Jersey by Alsop & Störmer Architects, in association with Mason Design Partnership, 1998. Reminiscent of a whale or upturned boat this curvilinear landmark structure provides a strong visual identity for the new Waterfront Development in Jersey.

right: The Soft and Hairy House, Tsukuba New Science City, Japan by Ushida Findlay, 1993. Among the surrealist and dream-like spaces of this house, the bubble-shaped bathroom interior brings a new dimension to the Japanese art of bathing. A swarm of tiny windows admit light like a cloud of rising bubbles.

such as the "living wall", which "like an organism allows elevations and depressions to grow out of itself", and like bones, allows convex and concave double curves with torsion between them. A living luminous quality was also sought via the use of transparent Lazur wall paints and stained glass.

Anthroposophic architecture has now grown into an international organic movement (perhaps one of the most coherent) with acclaimed work in Europe, USA, and Australia, and a network that hosts international conferences and exhibitions. Notable architects in Europe include Imre Makovecz (see page 166), Erik Asmussen (see page 100), Thomas Rau (see page 202), Ton Albert and Max van Huut, Joachim Eble, Christopher Day, and Camphill Architects. Working in this tradition outside Europe, are architects such as Thompson and Rose (USA), Denis Bowman (Canada), and Gregory Burgess (Australia – see page 110).

Being-like form

Another key Germanic influence was Hugo Häring. Although he produced important buildings, such as Garkau Farm, Lübeck, Germany, his real contribution lay in organic theory. In *Wege zur Form* (Approach to Form) he expressed his belief that every place and task implies a form, and that it is the architect's job to discover it and let it unfold. Function, he felt, was derived from nature and life whereas expression came from the human intellect. Functional forms are the same throughout the world and history, while expressive forms are bound by *Blut und Erkenntnis* (Blood and Knowledge) and thus dependent on time and place. He abhorred the trend in the 1920s, by such architects as Le Corbusier, to impose simplistic geometric forms from the outside and then justify them by their inherent beauty. Whereas a polished metal sphere may appeal to us intellectually, a flower, Häring felt, is an emotional experience and a

right: The Amsterdam headquarters of the ING Bank by Alberts and van Huut is one of the most ambitious projects based on anthroposophic principles. Ten organic-shaped towers are linked via an internal walkway that playfully twists and turns through the building. A wall sculpture reiterates this movement and reflects daylight into the interior.

higher order of expression. He spoke of buildings as *organhaft* (organ-like) exhibiting *Wesenhafte Gestalt* (being-like form). But although this did not automatically lead to curved rather than orthogonal shapes, it did lead away from the poverty and dominance of the straight line and right angle. Häring's ideas had a strong influence on architects such as Alvar Aalto, Louis Kahn, and his close friend Hans Scharoun.

The prolific projects of Hans Scharoun, one of the chief exponents of organic building in Germany, range from individual houses, apartment blocks, and schools to large-scale post-war re-developments in Berlin and other cities. He successfully translated Häring's concepts of organic functionalism into reality and went beyond this to develop new spatial experiences, as well as forms, based on careful research into site, functional needs, and deeper social meanings. In his best-known project, the Berlin Philharmonie, the radical arena auditorium places performers in the centre of the audience and embraces both within a free-ranging asymmetrical auditory space. By contrast, the adjacent Musical Institute takes on a more sober orthogonal design to reflect a concern with reason and knowledge. Scharoun had considerable influence on post-war Germany and the spirit continued through the work of Böhm, Behnisch, and Fehling & Gogel.

The passionate and playful brand of organic design, as exemplified by Gaudí and the Spanish Modernistas, continues to arise out of Latin culture and folk traditions. César Manrique of Lanzarote displayed a natural feeling for the organic: beauty of the site, local volcanic materials, vernacular forms, free and flowing spaces, and a mood of youth, spontaneity, and fun. Apart from being a talented artist, he had a deep commitment to nature and the culture and environment of his home, the small volcanic island in the Canary Islands. He spent his life warring against speculators and authorities responsible for environmental destruction and unbridled tourism. He raised local and international awareness of Canarian culture, its fragile wildlife habitats, and its vernacular architecture. The island, now a declared UNESCO World Heritage Site, has achieved much in protecting itself from the unrestricted spread of ubiquitous high-rise hotels and the worst ravages of tourism. Manrique was involved in the design of a series of imaginative public projects built to entertain (and educate) locals and visitors about different facets of Lanzarote's landscape, wildlife, and indigenous culture. They include Mirador del Rio, Jardín de Cactus, Jameos del Agua, and his former home, now the Fundación César Manrique.

At the foot of Mount Corona, Lanzarote, is a chain of petrified volcanic passages and bubble-like chambers. In part of this system César Manrique created his first architectural project: Jameos del Agua – a spectacular grotto, open to the sky, that contains spiral stairs and walkways, restaurants, bars, saltwater lagoon, and subterranean concert hall.

Dirty realism

While the American, Germanic, and Latin strands of organic architecture continued to evolve, a maverick modern movement – Deconstructivism – arose whose free-form products are sometimes confused with the organic tradition. Architects such as Frank O. Gehry, Peter Eisenman, Daniel Libeskind, Enric Miralles, Rem Koolhaas, Ben van Berkel, and Zaha Hadid have all set out, in their different ways, to displace order, harmony, hierarchy, and orthogonal form. Although their work shares some organic interests, such as the use of fractal geometry, it is driven by quite

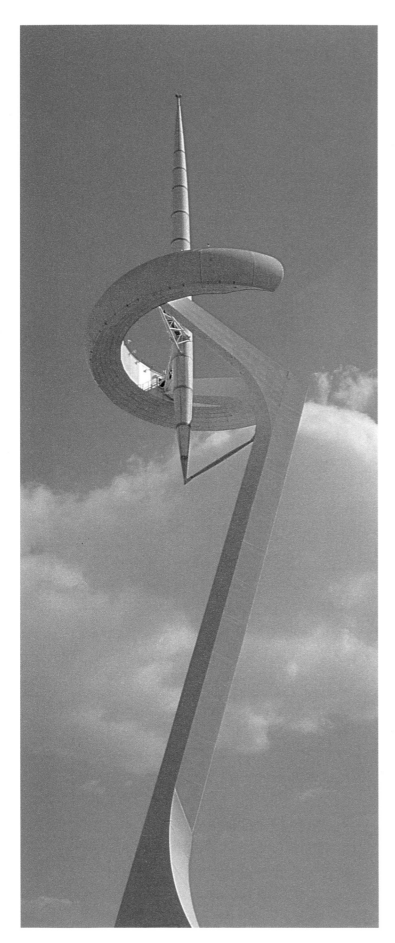

left: Based on Santiago Calatrava's concept of a kneeling figure making an offering, the Montjuïc Communications Tower was designed, in association with Arata Isozaki, for the 1992 Olympic Games. Its dynamic springing form has become a symbol of the progressive and artistic culture of Barcelona.

different imperatives. These stem from a hard intellectual view of the modern world, characterized by Gehry as "dirty realism". The contorted and fragmented forms of Deconstructivist buildings, full of sharp angles, dislocated spaces, and harsh, high-tech materials, all speak of a world of uncertainty and apprehension rather than one of organic holism, ecological design, and hope for humanity and the planet. However, elements of Gehry's later works, such as the gleaming roof of the Guggenheim Museum, Bilbao, Spain (page 53), that "unfolds" like the petals of a huge flower, do evoke positive feelings.

Deep organic, deep green

Mainstream architecture is also adopting outward organic forms. The stronghold of rectilinear design is under siege. Free-form design is on the attack. More liberated and imaginative forms, unacceptable to major corporate clients a few years ago, are now actively sought. Notable examples include the Bordeaux Law Courts and London's Millennium Dome (Sir Richard Rogers), the curvaceous London mayoral headquarters (Sir Norman Foster), the competition-winning elliptical dome for the Chinese national opera house and concert hall, Beijing (Paul Ardreau), the Media Centre, Lord's Cricket Ground, London, and the Earth Centre Ark, Doncaster, England (Future Systems).

But are these projects motivated by the spirit of organic design? Geometry and science are, once again, prime movers. The intellectual attraction of new science and the purity of geometric forms, made even more dazzling via three-dimensional modelling, are stimulating their use for their own sake. They are being applied as design imposed from the outside rather than organic design created, like life and nature, from within. Even fractal geometry, a deeper representation of natural relationships, is being applied externally, divorced from the internal functions of the building. The use of geometry and science, alone, does not produce organic design.

"Green" or sustainable architecture is evolving fast, too, but there is a danger that, instead of being the vanguard of a new, holistic architecture, it will become engrossed in high-tech and energy-saving issues. Few eco-architecture projects go beyond these parameters to explore the deeper world of spiritual expression and organic form where the wonder and sensual beauty of the natural world are combined with essential practical needs of economy, efficiency, and conservation. What is now coming, as the Breaking Wave, is a new architecture that expresses the union of organic inspiration and truly sustainable design.

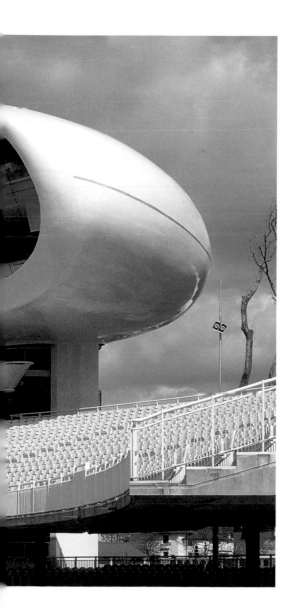

below; the curvaceous aluminium-cased monocoque shell of the Media Centre at Lord's Cricket Ground, London by Amanda Levete and Jan Kaplicky of Future Systems. Fabricated like a yacht hull, a Cornish boatbuilder was the main contractor for the superstructure.

Nature's forms

Patterns and forms in nature, such as the spiral and fractal, are products of internal laws of growth and of the action of external forces, such as sun, wind, and water. Architects learn to use natural forms from observing living structures: trees, bones, shells, wings, webs, eyes, petals, scales, and microscopic creatures – as illustrated in the following pages. They are the very forms of life and growth and have been key inspirations in organic architecture, whether for ornament, as in Art Nouveau, structure, as with Gaudí, or metaphor, as with Makovecz.

The dynamics of form

Pioneering students of nature's forms, whose influences are still felt today, included Johann Wolfgang von Goethe (1749–1832), Ernst Haeckel (1834–1919), and D'Arcy Wentworth Thompson (1860–1948). Goethe studied natural forms and coined the term *morphologie.* He also applied ideas of metamorphosis to art and architecture, the dynamics of form active in all living organisms, whereby an orderly and cyclic transformation can be traced in all plant forms from seed to calyx to blossom to fruit (and to seed again) – a concept central to the development of organic architecture (see page 40).

Biologist and zoologist Ernst Haeckel studied Radiolaria (plankton) and was captivated by their exquisite geometrical forms and complex patterns. He is best known for his work *Art Forms in Nature* with its magnificent illustrated plates by lithographer Adolf Giltsch. Such stunning illustrations had an immediate impact on Art Nouveau and the work of Hermann Obrist, August Endell, and Louis Comfort Tiffany. Architect René Binet not only produced a book of ornament based on Haeckel's illustrations, but also designed the monumental entrance gate to the 1900 Paris World Exposition, as a vast radiolarian. Haeckel, himself, used beautiful jellyfish forms as ceiling decoration in his former home, the "Villa Medusa".

"The shape is a result of the natural surroundings" says Michael Carmichael, creator of Noah's Ark, near Santa Barbara, California. "I wanted to leave the trees so I built around them." Looking like a giant armadillo or stranded whale, the house appears different from every angle. Similar to the form of a shell it has no walls or roof and, reminiscent of animal scales, its surface is entirely clad with rippling wooden shingles.

Zoologist D'Arcy Thompson also set out to define and classify form and studied an astounding range of natural forms from microscopic Radiolaria to shells, insect wings to raindrops, snowflakes to the splash of a pebble in a pond. His thoughtful results are published in his classic work *On Growth and Form* where he concludes that we must "…realise that in general no organic forms exist save such are in conformity with physical and mathematical laws".

Forms of the future

There is an upsurge in interest in nature's designs spurred on by modern science and mathematics and particularly amongst engineers, who are using new computer-modelling technology to twist, fold, and curve shapes to support stresses more elegantly. As science sees further into the microscopic world of matter and uncovers more about the remarkable structures of living things, nature continues to surprise us and teach us how we might build more cleverly, economically, subtly, and ecologically.

facing page; Peromedusae from the 1904 edition of *Art Forms in Nature* by Ernst Haeckel. Stunning visual images such as this brought a new understanding of the structure and evolution of organic life. They also had a strong influence on artists and architects connected with the development of Art Nouveau.

Please note: The comparisons between the natural forms and the architectural images shown on the following pages, have been used for illustration only and do not necessarily represent a conscious connection made by the architect.

left: Electron micrography has given access to a whole new world of images, structures, and patterns from nature to inspire the organic designer. Diatoms, such as this *Campylodisus hibernicus* (photographed at a magnification of 250 times life size), have exquisite intricately patterned glass-like cell walls, or frustules. Their double curved form, similar to a hyperbolic paraboloid, is fringed with radial rows of tiny holes or striae.

facing page: The concentric "petals" of
the Guggenheim Museum, Bilbao, Spain,
by Frank Gehry, echo the heart of a rose.

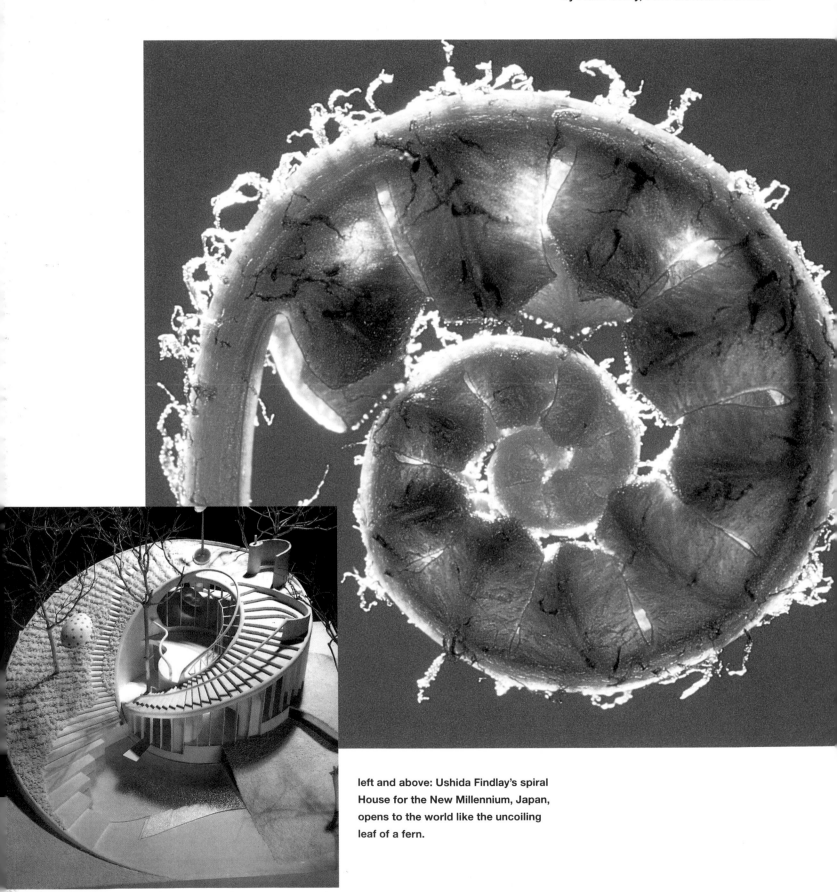

left and above: Ushida Findlay's spiral
House for the New Millennium, Japan,
opens to the world like the uncoiling
leaf of a fern.

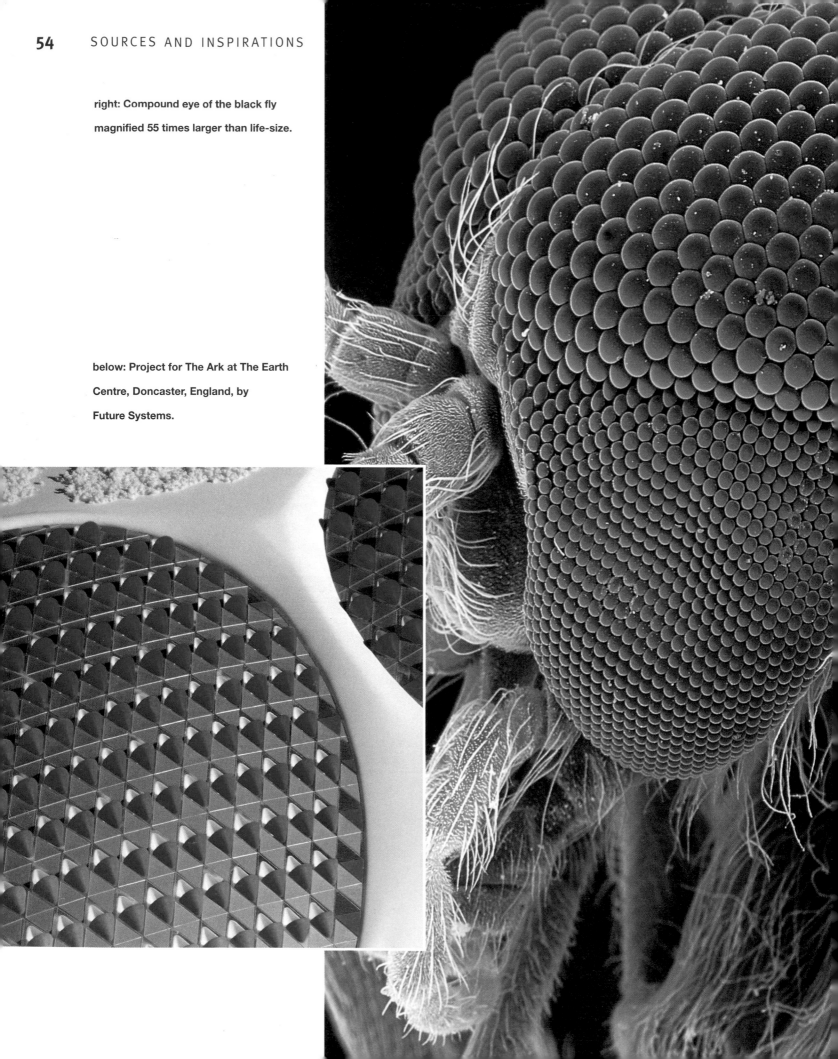

right: Compound eye of the black fly
magnified 55 times larger than life-size.

below: Project for The Ark at The Earth
Centre, Doncaster, England, by
Future Systems.

above: Domed roof of the Palazzetto dello Sport, Rome by Pier Luigi Nervi and Annibale Vitellozzi, 1956–7.

left: Spider's web.

left: Palm leaves.

below: Window detail from the Price
Residence, Corona del Mar, California,
1987, by Bart Prince.

right: Wing feathers of the varied thrush.

below:
Wings detail from the spire of the Roman
Catholic church, Szàzhalombàtta,
Hungary, by Imre Makovecz.

left: Close up of the scales of a pangolin.

inset left: Curving slate roof of the Roman Catholic church at Paks, Hungary, by Imre Makovecz.

near right: Detail of a green abalone shell from Baja California.

inset below: Detail of shingle roof of the Price Residence, Corona del Mar, California, by Bart Prince.

centre right: Crab shell.

inset centre right: Fish fin detail of "Ojo del Sol" (Eye of the Sun) house, Berkeley, California, by Eugene Tsui.

far right: Tidal patterns in beach sand, Cornwall, England.

inset far right: Organic design of the Ford "Ka".

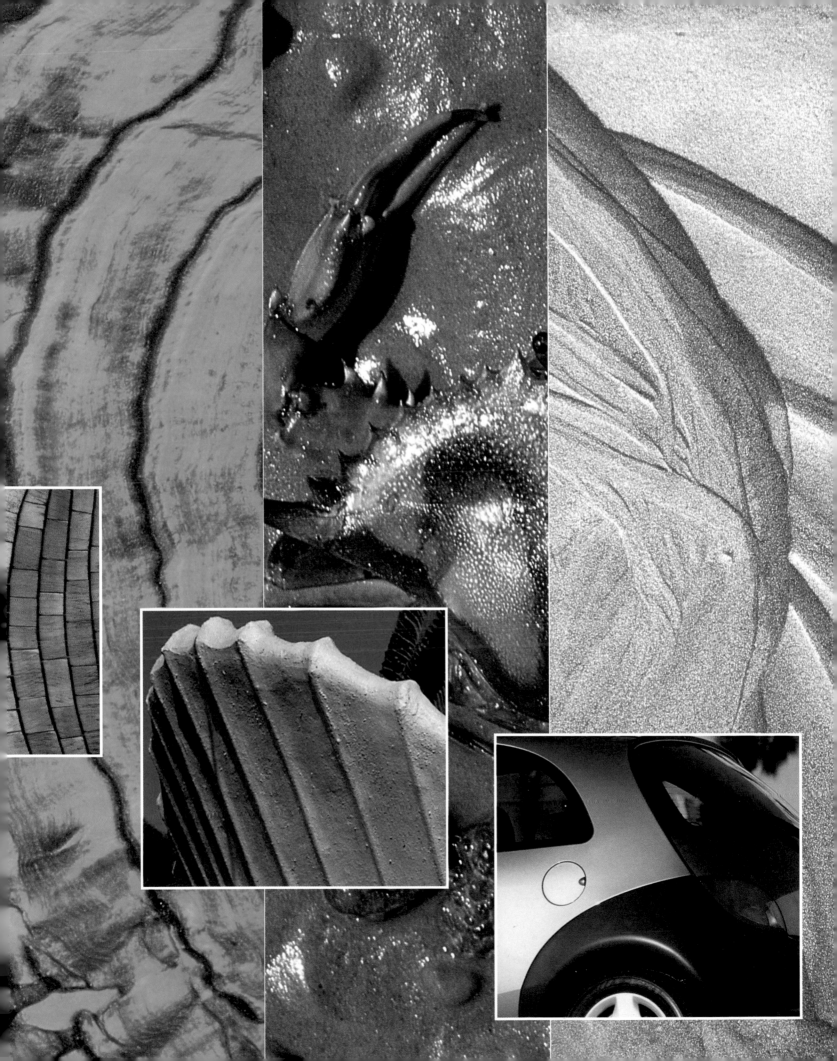

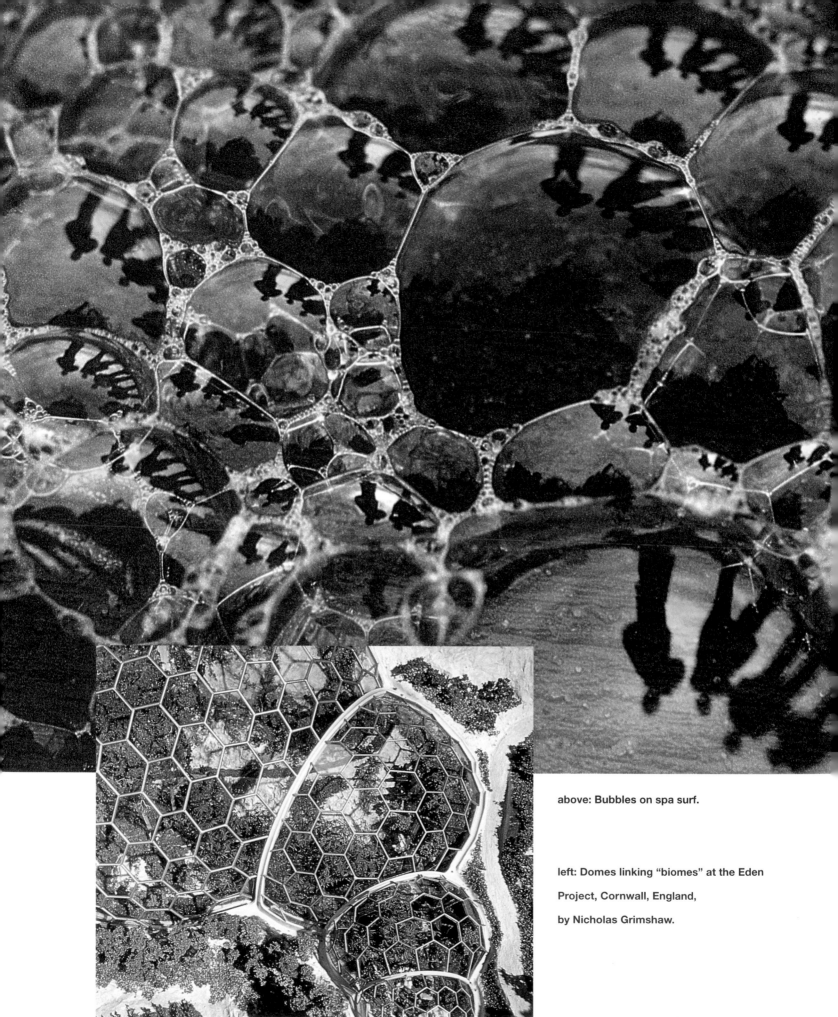

above: Bubbles on spa surf.

left: Domes linking "biomes" at the Eden
Project, Cornwall, England,
by Nicholas Grimshaw.

above:

Jack o' lantern fungus.

right:

Roof canopies at High Desert

home, Palm Springs, California,

by Kendrick Bangs Kellogg.

G e o m e t r y

In modern architecture, geometry is manifest more in materials, structures, and new mathematics than in notions of proportion and symmetry. Some of the greatest 20th century champions of non-rectilinear organic forms have been engineering pioneers such as Max Berg, Eugène Freyssinet, Robert Maillart, Pier Luigi Nervi, Félix Candela, and Buckminster Fuller. They pushed new geometry and new materials, such as reinforced concrete, to their limit to create daring and beautiful structures. Their search for structures to span ever wider spaces with less material led to a light, "floating" architecture that uses thin shell, frame, and tent constructions of audacious three-dimensional shapes using parabolic and hyperbolic curves, barrel vaults, folded slabs, and geodesic domes.

Today, detailed study of nature's forms, use of non-linear geometry, and computer modelling are exploring an exciting, and as yet, little-known world of new non-linear organic architecture. At a time when nature is viewed as being a mercurial mixture of order and chaos, pattern and accident, simplicity and complexity, it is not surprising that the creators of buildings should respond with new concepts.

Cecil Balmond of Ove Arup & Partners, London, specializes in what he calls "informal or exotic structures", based on new science, number systems, fractals, and powerful computer modelling systems. Discovering patterns hidden within numbers is the key to re-animating structural engineering in a process that he likens more to weaving and basketry than traditional engineering.

The lightweight timber gridshell, for example, is simple, economical, and strong, and uses sustainable materials. Like the catenary structures derived by Gaudí from his hanging models (see page 34), the thin wooden laths of the gridshell act like chains to take up optimum structural forms. Pioneered in the 1970s by Frei Otto for Germany's Mannheim Garden Festival, the gridshell has been chosen by Edward Cullinan Architects, working with Büro Happold, for the undulating tunnel structure of the Weald & Downland Open Air Museum, Sussex, England. Elsewhere, Philippe Samyn has evolved "harmonic" double curved structures, using fractals, which are low-cost, lightweight, and easy to erect (see page 212), Shoei Yoh uses local craftsmen to "weave" organic bamboo grids (see page 162), and Santiago Calatrava has engineered sculptural bridges (see page 66), roofs, and towers (see page 46) with great panache and elegance.

Boat design is also another example of an allied craft that employs specialist knowledge of complex double curved forms. Gehry used naval architecture computer software to model the fractal shapes of the Guggenheim Musem, Bilbao (see page 53) and Future Systems used boatbuilders to fabricate precision parts for the Media Centre at Lord's Cricket Ground, London (see page 47). Roofers familiar with domes were employed by Alsop & Störmer to detail the free-form "pods" at Peckham Library, London, and the hull-like La Frégate Café, Jersey, Channel Islands (see page 42).

Geometry and structural morphology are prime interests of Philippe Samyn. He is conducting a constant search for harmonic structures that are light and inexpensive such as this wooden lattice dome (see also page 210).

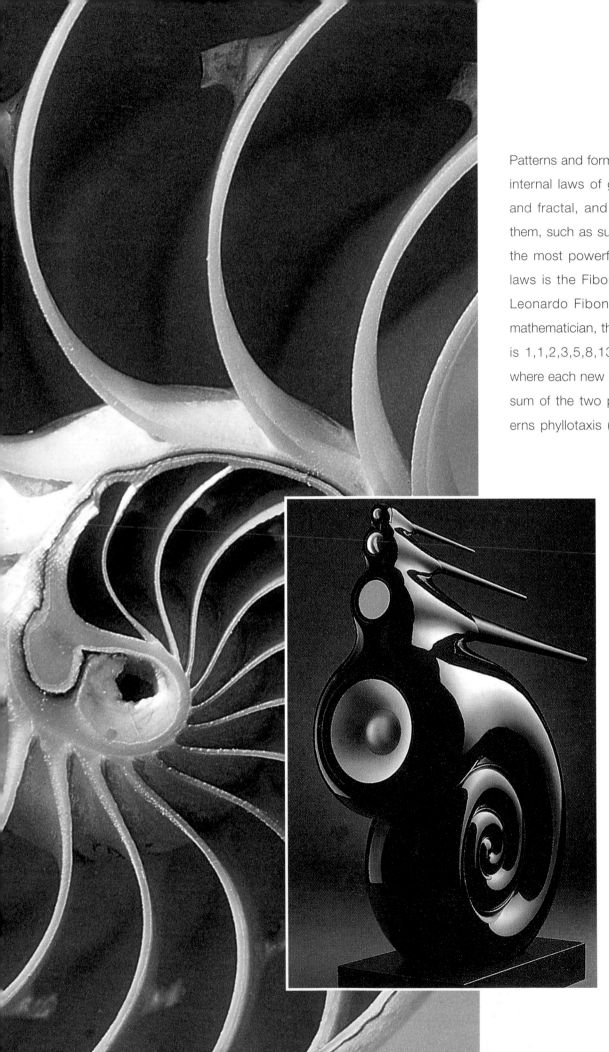

Spirals

Patterns and forms in nature are products of internal laws of growth, such as the spiral and fractal, and external forces acting on them, such as sun, wind, and water. One of the most powerful and widespread natural laws is the Fibonacci series. Named after Leonardo Fibonacci, the medieval Italian mathematician, the infinite number sequence is 1,1,2,3,5,8,13,21,34,55,89 and so on, where each new number is generated by the sum of the two preceding numbers. It governs phyllotaxis (the arrangement of leaves

far left: Section through a nautilus shell.

left: The Nautilus™ high-fidelity speaker by B&W Products.

facing page above: Spiral staircase at the Jardín de Cactus, Lanzarote, by César Manrique.

facing page right: Interior spiral ramp of small tower at the Solomon R. Guggenheim Museum, New York, by Frank Lloyd Wright.

on a stem) to give optimum chlorophyll production. It also describes spiral growth patterns of objects as diverse as pineapples, sunflowers, pine cones, seeds, tendrils of climbing plants, animal horns, and numerous shells, the most often cited being the nautilus. The number series generates the Golden Section, the ratio of 1:1168 or 8:13, and the Golden Rectangle, whose sides are in that ratio. This ratio was held by Classical and Renaissance architects to create harmonious proportions. Furthermore, arcs drawn with the radii of the squares in larger and larger golden rectangles will generate a continuous logarithmic spiral.

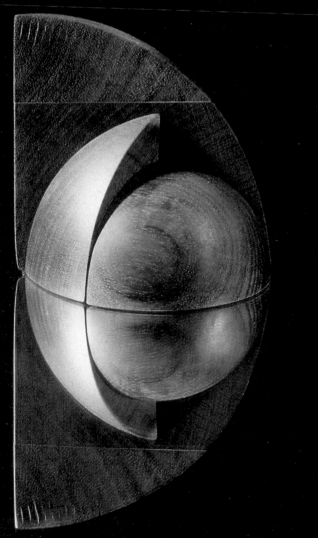

Curves

If according to Dutch architect Ton Albert "every angle has its angel", then surely every curve must have its archangel! According to Gaudí "curves are for God". The circle representing the path of the sun, moon, and stars, and the cycle of life and death, has been used since pre-historic times for the henges and barrows of sacred sites. Domes, arches, and vaults were used in religious architecture because of their power to evoke the sublime. Even in secular use curves can still retain a special emotional power. Curves may be gentle and graceful like the swan-neck or S-curve of life, so prevalent in decorative designs using plant motifs, or they may be tense and explosive like a coiled spring. They may also be sleek and streamlined to respond to the energy and force of wind and water, or sensual and erotic in suggesting the beauty of living forms. Curves are very strong and can reach optimum structural shapes as parabolic and hyperbolic arches and shells.

above left: Twin inclined and split arches of Bach De Roda-Felip 11 Bridge, Barcelona, by Santiago Calatrava.

left: Ovals, spheres, and quadrants are mirrored in a reflecting pond. Wooden model of the Museum for Musical Instruments and Crafts, Flanders, Belgium, by Philippe Samyn.

right: Parabolic brick arches support the roof terrace above on the top floor of the Casa Milà, Barcelona, by Antoni Gaudí.

Fractals and iterative systems

When in the 1970s Benoit Mandelbrot coined the term fractal, in his groundbreaking book *The Fractal Geometry of Nature*, he fundamentally changed the way we look at the natural world. Central to the concept is that of self-similarity – from the macro to micro scales. However far you zoom in or zoom out of a fractal system there will always be an unending cascade of self-similar, but not identical, detail. Fractal geometry describes natural shapes and rhythms such as snowflakes, leaves, tree branches, mountains, waves, and coastlines. Applied to architecture, rhythm and composition become fractal self-similar detail, often referred to as "textural progression". From a fractal point-of-view, Modern Movement architecture lacks textural progression and harmony with its surroundings, while the work of Frank Lloyd Wright, and other organic architects, show fine fractal cascades of detail from the large (plans and elevations) to the small (windows, doors, and decorative patterns). As Mandelbrot commented: "A Mies van der Rohe building is a scale-bound throwback to Euclid, while a high period Beaux Arts building is rich in fractal aspects." Fractal geometry opens up endless possibilities for designers interested in expressing the more complex underlying rhythms and random patterns of nature. As music has been found to display fractal distributions, it is even possible to use music to generate natural organic designs.

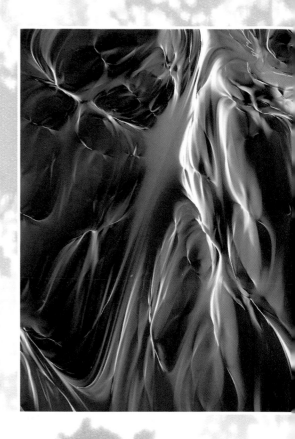

background and right: Iterative details of a Mandelbrot set. "Why is geometry often called cold and dry? One reason lies in its inability to describe the shape of a cloud, a mountain, a coastline, or a tree. Clouds are not spheres, mountains are not cones, coastlines are not circles, and bark is not smooth, nor does lightning travel in straight lines." Benoit Mandelbrot, *The Fractal Geometry of Nature*.

below: Frank Lloyd Wright, Ennis House.
inset: "Tex-tile" detail from the façade.

above: Proposed extension to the Victoria and Albert Museum, London, by Daniel Libeskind.

inset: "Fractile" detail from exterior surface.

Environment

Rectilinear buildings are not ideal "green" buildings. While buildings are mostly still linear, the physical laws governing the dynamics of fluids, heat, light, sound, and force are mostly non-linear. The processes of growth and decay occur, not in straight lines, but in curves and cycles. Yet we continue to design and build rectilinear straightjackets that constrain and block natural energy flows. Curvilinear buildings, on the other hand, work with nature and allow optimum shapes and forms to be developed that are more efficient, economic, and appropriate to local climate and environmental conditions.

It is well known that wind flows, for instance, are best responded to with curved aerodynamic forms that reduce "drag" as seen in the smooth curving profiles of modern cars and planes. Passive ventilation, to avoid or reduce energy-hungry air-conditioning, is also enhanced by aerodynamic shapes (see the wind towers at Bluewater Mall, page 74). Why then are architects and engineers so slow to bring these benefits to the world of building?

The sun moves in a semicircular path across the sky and yet most buildings are rectangular – their orientation, layout, and straight façades limiting the full benefits of natural lighting and passive solar gain. For cooler climates, however, a curving sun-facing façade, which catches the sun throughout the day and the seasons, seems the obvious solution. If feasible, it would be even better if rooms, or even entire buildings, could slowly revolve, ecologically powered, like a garden summerhouse, to track the sun or shade according to the climate or season.

Temperature flows also behave better in curvilinear interiors. Heat is more evenly distributed avoiding corner hot and cold spots. Heat is most efficiently conserved within a compact form, the sphere being the most efficient. Ventilation flows are more easily controlled bringing an altogether more equitable and comfortable indoor climate. In harsh climates, semi-underground earth-sheltered structures can produce zero-energy buildings – ideally suited to organic design.

Daringly cantilevered over a waterfall, Fallingwater at Bear Run, Pennsylvania, Frank Lloyd Wright's famous design, seems to grow out of the site and reflect the rhythm of the upwardly rising rock ledges.

The shapes and forms of internal spaces affect our feelings. Maybe because natural forms have many positive associations, they evoke feelings of harmony and wellbeing. In esoteric terms, curvilinear structures and forms are said to produce different subtle energy resonances. According to ecological designer and teacher Victor Papanek: "On a near-mystic level, various sensory and subconscious triggers released by such structures flood our minds with a sense of joy and wellbeing."

In the past, organic architecture has not always used the "greenest" materials. But this is changing and many more organic buildings are now being designed with an increased ecological awareness to incorporate low-energy, sustainable, and recycled materials and energy-saving systems.

In conclusion

We have come full circle to consider the future of organic architecture and design. In my first book *The Natural House Book* (revised as *The New Natural House Book*), I proposed a Gaia Charter for design to satisfy the three themes of Health, Ecology, and Spirit. What is now needed is an integration of these themes with the philosophy and power of organic architecture.

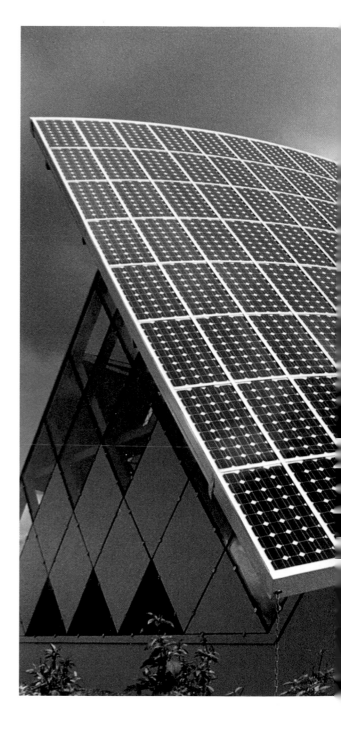

The Gaia Charter for organic architecture and design

Let the design:

• **be inspired by nature and be sustainable, healthy, conserving, and diverse**

• **unfold, like an organism, from the seed within**

• **exist in the "continuous present" and "begin again and again"**

• **follow the flows and be flexible and adaptable**

• **satisfy social, physical, and spiritual needs**

• **"grow out of the site" and be unique**

• **celebrate the spirit of youth, play, and surprise**

• **express the rhythm of music and the power of dance.**

Light

left: Photo-voltaic array at the Baglan Energy Park, South Wales, harnesses light as a clean energy source.

below: The interplay of areas brightness and shadow makes use of light as an architectural feature.

above: Wind farm in Northern California.

left: Wind towers at the Bluewater Mall, Kent, England, by Battle McCarthy, M & E Consultants, and Eric Kuhne Architects.

Wind and Earth

below: Volcanic rock bridge over the

pool at the Fundación César

Manrique, Lanzarote.

Water

left: One of the many beautiful water sculptures found placed along the elevated walkway linking the ten office towers of the ING Bank HQ, Amsterdam, by Albert and van Huut.

left: The meander patterns of this water sculpture in the grounds of the Rudolf Steiner Seminary, Järna, Sweden, celebrate a natural spring source.

below: Like a great ship at anchor, the green organic shape of the Museum of Science and Technology, Amsterdam, by Renzo Piano, captures the spirit of the waterfront location.

Materials

left: The curvilinear forms of the walls and walkways at the Canadian Museum of Civilization by Douglas Cardinal are constructed in brick.

near right: A fine staircase by Dan Liebermann is a perfect expression of the organic use of wood.

far right: The American Patrick Dougherty makes extraordinary structures from woven willow. This giant staddle stone shelter stands at the entrance to Compton Verney House, Warwickshire, England. Dougherty's structures have a life of their own once they sprout and grow. Some are allowed to go their own way, others are commissioned as short-term structures, then taken down and composted.

part 2

living organic architecture

Part 2 is about "living" organic architecture. It represents a cross-section of practising organic architects and their architecture – the first time such a broad compilation has been made. Featured here is the work of 30 architects from 15 countries giving a truly diverse and international perspective. All of the architects have been invited to make personal statements in their own words about their individual design approach. Some architects are internationally famous while others are lesser known. In some cases, one building has been selected, while in others, a number of projects are shown. The majority of the architects have specialized in organic architecture for all, or most, of their working life. Some architects, however, have more recently broadened their usual design vocabulary to include notable non-rectilinear designs. This may be an isolated event or a new trend. It may also indicate a move, in some of the larger international architectural and engineering practices, away from an emphasis on orthogonal design and towards exploration of more free form and curvilinear designs. Some free form design can be criticized, rather like Art Nouveau, as merely applying trendy surface styling to conventional designs. These tentative steps may, however, be the precursor to a more profound change in design direction that could radically affect mainstream architecture.

Most architects featured, however, are male! This is not a reflection on the organic field per se but on architecture, engineering, and design fields in general which continue to be male dominated. It is only to be hoped that, not only will more women join these professions, but that many of these will also become talented organic designers. There is a natural link between organic design and ecological design that remains largely unexplored and unexpressed. This is one of the most exciting avenues for new architecture and design, full of fresh inspirations and solutions, only waiting for new explorers to venture into this uncharted region.

The profiles have purposely not been arranged alphabetically, chronologically, or geographically but organically to display the vitality, contrast, and diversity of the architects' approach and their work. Neither have they been categorized into "types" or "styles" of organic design. Most organic architects strongly resist their work being pigeonholed as this usually leads to misunderstandings. It is far better for every reader to respond in his or her own way and, better still, to go and experience organic buildings first hand, without preconceptions and using all their senses.

Fabrizio Carola

building for people

The starting point of any piece of architecture should be the human being. This must be considered before any of the other practical, material or financial considerations. Buildings are not for architects, they are for the people that will live and work within them, and every building must be in tune with those for whom it is intended. And this must take into account how humans vary in thousands of different ways, how people have evolved and live in completely different contexts. So, right at the beginning of any proposed project, an architect must get to know the context. Only then will we be able to build for specific people and situations.

Working from this starting point you will discover that a mental process of analysis and synthesis follows the birth of any idea. This mental process guides the choice of appropriate techniques within a specific context, but the analysis is not necessarily scientific and rational, there is also an important intuitive component. Intuition in fact plays a large part in the whole process because it brings into play a non-rational ingredient which places the work nearer to the architect. You could say that intuition introduces a poetic dimension. I believe that this irrational aspect brings to the process those facts which are very real but which cannot be reduced to statistics and measurement in degrees, metres, kilogrammes or dollars. Without this poetic ingredient buildings are merely sterile machines for living in.

Architecture should not resort to pure fantasy, it is not a game to amuse the architect, but rather the concrete result of a process which is half rational and half intuitive. The mental process involved in creating a piece of architecture is basically exactly the same process as that which, in one form or another, is at the roots of all inventions throughout history, the foundation of all works and discoveries which are humanity's heritage.

In my personal experience – which I do not suggest is necessarily true for everyone – I find that there are three stages in the creation of a project. The

The Kaedi hospital, Mauritania, 1984. The principal characteristics of this project are both the materials and the groundplan. I wanted to avoid reinforced concrete because cement and iron are imported, and because reinforced concrete responds very badly to the heat and the Sahelian climate. I also wanted to avoid wood because Mauritania is a region on the way to desertification. The remaining choices were local materials of sand, stone, and earth. I had at my disposal a large quantity of rice balls (the waste from cleaning rice), which are useless for building but makes very good fuel. I was able to use this waste to heat kilns and make fired bricks from the earth. I built a factory where we produced two and a half million earth bricks for the main construction of the hospital.

As part of the plan I wanted to create a permanent contact between the patient and his family: what I call "familiotherapy". The design developed to allow families to camp near the patients so they could support them emotionally as well as in practical ways. For that purpose the rooms have two doors, one going into the main arched corridor which is technically reserved for doctors and medical staff, the other door opening onto the garden giving families easy access and allowing them to be near the patients.

The Herbal Market, Bamako, Mali, 1996. This market of 20 stands for selling medicinal herbs was constructed from stone and fired bricks. It is grouped around a central courtyard. The project was created for the Institute of Traditional Medicine of Bamako with funding from the Ministry of Health and Terranuova.

first stage is the conscious and rational analysis of the given theme, where all the facts and the problems can be listed, analysed and taken into account. This is a rational look at the project. The second stage of the process is non-rational, the subconscious and intuitive assessment. At this point the subconscious, having assimilated all the facts it has been given, is often able to influence the project by bringing its inner knowledge and experience into play to suggest a solution that could not be obtained simply through rational processes. It is principally in this phase that artistic influences come to the fore. The third stage is rational and conscious once more, and consists of evaluation and technical assessment of the solutions proposed by the subconscious.

Analysis-synthesis is a simple process of question and answer. But unfortunately the process is too often ignored. For example, no one applied it when Europe transplanted a specific style of architecture to Africa, a style which corresponded with European needs but had nothing at all to do with African requirements. Instead of analysing and then synthesizing the African context with the aim of obtaining an African solution, responding to African facts, a limited northern European result was exported which arose from a totally different context – provoking cultural disaster.

Some people are the creators of civilization, others are simply the users – and they often use it extremely badly. When western civilization was introduced to or imposed upon Africa through the power of arms or dollars, it was not brought by the makers of civilization such as Galileo or Leonardo, Mozart or Einstein, but by mere users. They imported with them what they knew from home, what they were used to using. Sadly, what they brought were often the least creative and most mediocre examples of our civilization. The Africans, for their part, trusted everyone who represented western civilization, so they passively adopted the false European architecture that was given to them, even though it failed to correspond to their needs. Moreover, this architecture additionally denied everything which belonged to their own tradition which had developed over thousands of years of real experiences and objective facts.

Regional Centre for Traditional Medicine (CRMT), Bandiagara, Mali, 1988. Stone was used because it is the traditional building material of the Dogon people of the region, whose traditional medicine the Centre was set up to research.

When we operate in our own country, where we were born and have grown up, in the environment where we are entirely at home through our birth, education and culture, we automatically take account of all the cultural ideas which are ingrained in us, they are completely familiar and natural. But when we change the environment, even the continent, and perhaps go into societies and cultures completely different from our own, we must be particularly attentive because things which may seem quite mundane and normal to us are often not at all as they appear. We must scrutinize our notion of the familiar, when it is applied in a different environment, so it doesn't lead us to create an unnatural monstrosity.

And this of course, is valid not only for architecture but for all activities. The method that I use to defend myself against this danger of creating monsters consists of trying to clear preconceptions from my memory. If, for example, I want to conceive a hospital, I do not go and consult images of existing hospitals. On the contrary, I try to forget all that I have ever known about hospitals. Then I recompose the notion of the hospital in a specific place, resulting directly from the real facts of the situation: the sun, the climate, economic and social conditions, the estimated budget, the materials, the available manpower and so on, and of course the specific requirements of the users. I use all these pieces to put the puzzle together, and I trust that it gives me an appropriate image for the place and the time.

Fabrizio Carola, Italy

Bart Prince

inside out

left: Prince residence,
Albuquerque, New
Mexico, 1989. View of
the east end of the
guest bedroom, built in
stucco, wood, glass,
and masonry.
below left and right:
Gradow/Benton
residence, Aspen,
Colorado, 1993.

The building designs that I have created result from the combination of creative responses to the various requirements of the program. By this I mean responses to everything from the initial requirements of the client, including intended budget and space needs, to the impact of the climate and the characteristics of the site. An analysis of these must come before any thoughts of design, form or structure. This is working from the inside out.

When I first meet clients I am interested in knowing their thoughts about the project, which usually initially consists of the general idea of what kinds of spaces they need and how they relate to each other. We don't talk about the look of the building or the shape at this stage, because these are things that must come as a result of the understanding of all aspects of the project once they are discovered and digested. I usually ask a client to give me a list of requirements which includes simple things such as number of bedrooms and other required spaces, as well as any preferences for or against materials, colors and so on.

We visit the site together right at the beginning of the process so I can discuss with them the importance of the impact of all the natural features, as well as any manmade characteristics such as adjacent buildings, streets, and utilities. We walk the site and talk about the climate, drainage, sun angles, views and any other aspects of the terrain and vegetation that will have an impact on the design and use of the resulting structure. During this process I make my own

Price residence, Corona del Mar, California, 1987. Built on a stunning site overlooking the ocean, the flowing motifs and materials reflect the proximity to the sea. The focus of the design, however, was more on the internal spaces rather than toward the ocean as requested by the clients. Despite the openness of the interior, it is surprisingly private.

observations about what I might call the nature or essence of the place as it might affect the design process. Other factors such as setbacks, height restrictions and other code requirements come into the process as well. I will usually return to the site by myself several times after this to fully understand the qualities I consider will impact on the eventual design. I will walk the site, and without preconceiving any kind of form, will imagine myself in any of the needed spaces and think where they would best be located both laterally on the property and at what elevation above the ground. I will think, for example, if I were in the living room at various times of the day, given the surroundings and special qualities I have discovered about the site, where it should best be located. I'll do the same in my mind for all the spaces in the building project and consider how each is to be related to the others. At this point they are simply imagined volumes of space with no physical separation or supporting structure. From here an idea begins to take shape for the work of architecture which will eventually define these spaces.

Once this information has been digested and organized in my mind I can begin to think about the possible organization of the space. This includes the space which will be enclosed which will be considered to be the "building," as well as the "resulting space" outside. In other words the "building" is not considered as an "object" which is set onto the site but rather more as something that grows out of the land as an integral response to the various requirements. Thus, architecture is not merely a form as considered from the exterior as an elevation or series of elevations, but rather as an enclosure of space by means of structure and materials which are consistent with the types of uses defined by them.

When a building is designed from the outside as an object rather than as something growing from the site we usually find that the functions are "stuffed" into it in whatever fashion that will not disturb the preconceived form. This is not a building that is responsive to the site but rather applied to it. When the great American architect Louis Sullivan talked

right: Mead/Penhall residence, Albuquerque, New Mexico, 1992, employs a wood-framed structure with galvanized metal and stucco finishes over a sand-blasted masonry base.
below: The Hight house, Mendocino, California.

about form following function I think he was often misunderstood. I take this to mean that form comes after, or results from the function, rather than as a preconception of what the building is going to look like before the understanding and organization of the function has been considered. Some architects have taken Sullivan's statement to mean that there is only one form that will express any given function, and have missed the implications of the connection of the whole idea to the site as an integral part of the design process.

I have been asked where my forms come from, as though there is an outside source and the forms are

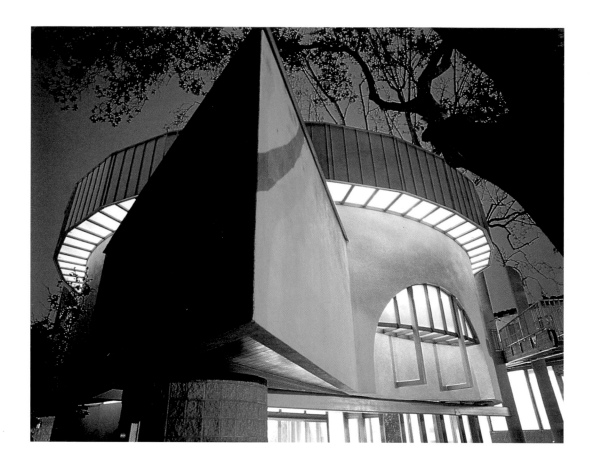

left: The exterior of the cantilevered art storage and main gallery and living space of the Spence residence, South Pasadena, California, 1989.

below: The entrance to the Spence residence.

a kind of kit of parts to be fitted together for any given design problem. But the form comes out of, or results from, the process of solving the problem. Any given design problem has a number of solutions. There is never only one solution that will work. When the form is allowed to grow from the implications of the program and the site, the result will be much more unusual and unexpected than anything that could be preconceived and applied to it.

I have had people say to me that my buildings look like something in nature that they think they can recognize. For example to some the Hight house in Mendocino looks like ocean waves or rolling hills. Others have said they think it's like a whale in motion. These associations are fine by me as it is human nature to associate something that has not been seen before with something else that is familiar. These people are, however, also likely to assume that I must have been trying to make it look like what they think they saw.

I would never want to start with the idea that the building was going to look like anything else, because this is applying a form from the outside rather than arriving at it from the inside, which to my mind is as bad as copying the outworn

Ruther residence, Santa Fe, New Mexico, 1993. The exterior stairway leads to the entrance and roof terrace.

styles of the past which no longer have anything to do with how we live. The form of the Mendocino house, for example, came about due to my understanding of the nature of the site and grew from it as a plant might, in the sense that it belongs there and would not have come into being in this form in any other location.

I am interested in creating works for our own time. They should express our lives and the age in which we are living which means they will have to be different from the buildings which have been built by our ancestors. We can of course learn from all that has been done by others who have done creative work before us, but we have to begin again each time we create a building under the sun.

Bart Prince, USA

creative urgency

Jacques Gillet

I need to create. I need to make new work, original work, made with my own hands in the open air. And that's why I do it. I make architecture in the way a sculptor makes sculpture or the painter creates paintings. I don't need a specific function to justify what I do. The function, for me, is in the doing.

I work with time. I deal with material and space and I bring it about in the course of time, using the density of time as a raw material. Only work that takes time has worth in my eyes. Only works that take time acquire the depth I long for. Time is a spiritual value, it is a factor that must be taken into account.

The Experimental Permanent Building Site of Sculpture-Architecture (PEBSA) at Ouffet, Belgium.
above and top right: design for the steel superstructure, 1997.
far right: outside the basement, 1992.
right: hands-on wood forms, 1987.

right: Preliminary sketch for the PEBSA project.

I draw what I hear and I see in Architecture the image of a resurrection. It takes root in the depth of the soil and climbs towards the light. It braces itself against the slope, then from the fertile east it springs and shows the dazzling sunset. The seed of the butterfly tree does what's left – it bursts out, germinates, grows tall, blooms, flies away but returns close to me, reassembled, to where I am sitting working in contemplation and gratitude. I hope.

Ouffet

Synthesis of arts is my passion. Architecture, sculpture, and painting are one and always have been throughout history. The Experimental Permanent Building Site of Sculpture-Architecture (PEBSA) at Ouffet illustrates some of the possibilities and the intended aims of experiment and evolution, while remaining centred on the creative research of a vivid and organic sculpture-architecture.

My students are the origin of the Ouffet project, for which I did the working drawings in 1979. They enjoyed creative direct "hands-on" work in the open air on a building site, and I wanted to go beyond the ephemeral aspects of their beautiful experiments to create a lasting work. So in 1976 I bought the site of an old quarry at Ouffet and in 1979 obtained permission for building in a "zone artisanale".

The site was to include workshops, storage and accommodation.

I started the hands-on building in spring 1980, taking the levels, digging trenches for drainage and pipes. Steel reinforcing and wood forms for the concrete began that summer, working first alone, then with a few students. The first concrete pouring took place in the autumn of 1980, in a great hurry before term began. During the school year we found little time or opportunity to come on the site. From 1980 till 1988 the floors and walls of the basement were gradually constructed of poured-in concrete. Volunteer students joined us who were incredibly committed to the project. The intermittent character of the project was relevant, the work was spread out and this had great value.

The relief wood forms I made in the early stages are more than ornament, they describe a way of working, a particular method of creating form as well as an architectural sculpture, a synthesis of the arts. Later on the forms will be enhanced by painting them.

Building alone was the first way of working, and it was an essential experiment. I retain, paradoxically, delight in the fire of action, of creation, in the very instant. This delight keeps one young. The second way of working was with the students. This is a passionate exchange above everything else, provoking discourse until exhaustion! We must hang on to that passion of youth. Great artistic insights and human wellbeing result from that way of working, with profound and lasting effects.

But I wanted to speed up the process, so I entered the third way of working. This involved living on site with the contractor's men, and working with them every day from dawn till dusk for several weeks, making the slab which covers the basement. This may be a faster process, but then perhaps it is not if you take into account the length of preparation time –

numerous detailed working drawings and models – plus all the time to put everything into order afterwards: not only the site, but also health and finances.

At my retirement came the fourth way of working. In a lightning transformation, rather than the slow and gradual progression of erecting forms and portions of the structure, entire walls and pillars have been mounted on the building site after fabrication in a steel construction factory. From earlier 5 cm (2 in) thin concrete shells we now got down to $1/2$ cm ($1/4$ in) thin steel sheet which allows exact reproduction of the model structure. Not only size and shape but light and shade, reflections, everything is there. Steel provides all the form at once, as well as colour. For me form is everything, like in pure music. Form is its own substance.

The work at Ouffet evokes a predominantly enthusiastic and positive response from all who experience it and all who have been involved in any way. The work belongs to everyone who has believed in it, and I thank them from my heart, thank them for their courage for 'the cause of Architecture', for Art, and for Life.

Jacques Gillet, Belgium

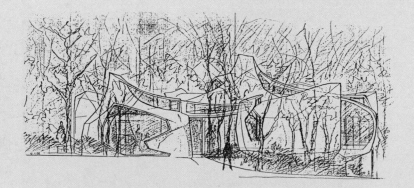

The Sculpture House, near Liège, designed and made in collaboration with sculptor Felix Roulin and engineer René Greisch, 1968. A free-form armature of metal rods covered with gunite, the building combines organic shapes, high thermal efficiency, fluid interior spaces, and maximum light.

with all the senses

Erik Asmussen

Ormen Långe, the pupils' home at the Steiner community at Järna, Sweden, appears at first to be a single-loaded long corridor building but it contains a surprising amount of spatial variety as well as diverse dwelling units. The perceived length is broken up into three articulated segments.

When looking at anthroposophic architecture people often want to know what the philosophy is behind the "form language". They speculate that there must be some sort of recipe providing a common denominator in anthroposophic architecture.

Fortunately, Rudolf Steiner did not suggest such a thing, though he clearly wanted to express something strongly in his architecture, as in all his art.

The expression, or the message, is reached through the very experiencing of the form language. Art should not be explained, but experienced by the senses. Steiner says, as did Goethe, that the justification of all art, including architecture, is that it allows one to express something which cannot be better conveyed in any other way. But architecture is not one of the free art forms. It is tied to its primary function of creating an environment for other activities.

below: The foyer of the Culture House at Järna is a fluid dynamic space designed for spontaneous activities suggested by the varied qualities of the space.

right: Exterior corridors of Ormen Långe are supported by tree-like wooden columns.

As I understand it, the goal for anthroposophic architecture is to strive to create a stimulating environment, which through its special atmosphere can act as an inspiration for the activity the building is intended for. At the same time as wishing to reflect the function in the form, one works continuously with organic forms. In his architecture Rudolf Steiner used the rules for development of the forms in the organic world, which Goethe illustrated in his metamorphosis doctrine. This is not an imitation of nature, but forms slowly emerge and transform according to the same rules that govern organic nature. The process-like transition, or the sharp turn which in different ways link polarized expressions of form, is characteristic and exists parallel in Goethanistic architecture and in nature.

When we were given the task of shaping the physical environment round the Rudolf Steiner seminary in Järna, the problem was both landscaping and building. The individual buildings' silhouettes looked to reflect the structure of the landscape. The building materials had to unify the building development and link with the traditional buildings already on the site. We unified individual buildings through materials, motifs and concepts. The form language and several other basic ideas developed while the first buildings were being designed. A visitor should be able to follow a process in which different concepts are repeated from building to building, but always in a new form adapted to a new situation.

Repeated elements include the fact all buildings feature a large room, bay windows, and a visible external staircase. The pupils' home, Ormen Långe, has a more porous structure than other buildings with a deep roof overhang and open external stairs leading to an open access gallery on the outside of the building. Studying demands a degree of isolation from the outer world. The pupils live in a type of collective group, expressed in the openness of the building to the outside world, with all circulation visible on the outside of the building. They also each have a private room. The lower parts of all the buildings at Järna contain living accommodation and the high parts rooms for communal use. Rudolf Steiner typically differentiates the upper and lower parts of a building, and frequently also encourages concave and convex forms to emerge strongly, perfectly adapted to the building materials. When designing a building in the office, we start with model studies, beginning with small scale site studies at 1:1000 or 1:400. New models and plans continuously correct each other. We consider that model studies are important at all stages, since architecture is three dimensional.

Most important of all is that architects and those that visit, use or live in the buildings should experience the architecture with all the senses at the same time – and this must include a sense of humour.

Erik Asmussen, Sweden

from catalogue *The Architecture of Erik Asmussen in Järna,* August 1987

left: Almandinen, the music building at Järna, plays with circles and polygons, straight lines and curves. Its rounded head is joined to the single-storey tail by the diagonal stairwell.

right: Window seats in the Music Room, a large light-filled space which contrasts with darker interior spaces in the building.

organic process

Douglas Cardinal

Curvilinear, organic buildings are often nowadays categorized as an indigenous Canadian style of architecture.

The method by which my buildings come into being is an
organic process where the shape and form of each room
is "wrapped" around its function. Thus the building
begins with the particular, with its individual functions, but
develops into a complete organism.

this page and overleaf: In Douglas Cardinal's own residence, bricks are joined into exuberant loops and curving forms. Glass provides a feeling of maximum integration with the elements. One aim of all his architecture is that the structures should mirror the flowing lines found in nature. He uses complex technology to assist in creating the sinuous gracious curves and organic shapes typical of his work.

Once the shape of a room is determined by its function, the room may be understood to act much like a single cell, with its own genetic code. Through the use of diagrams, area relationships are planned between the individual "cells", eventually to create a matrix of rooms. With this matrix the building begins to design itself. Through a natural and organic process, a spinal cord develops as the rooms, or cells, form into clusters of relationships. In this initial stage the design is quite flexible as the cells in the cord may be rearranged in endless variations.

Gradually the relationships between the functions of the organism evolve. Once these relationships are tested and analysed by the potential inhabitants of the building, the building is transported onto the site, where the natural elements, such as the wind and sun angles, will shape the building from the outside in. A balance must be achieved between the external and internal elements which shape the building, much like a tree which has its own genetic code but which is also shaped by the natural forces acting upon it.

When the form of the entire organism is defined, images that give an aesthetic expression to the character of the building are incorporated into the design. The exterior shell of the building then becomes a sculptural expression of the themes and ideas of the design, and of its internal environment. In this way the organic process, the internal and the external, binds together to create a work of architecture.

Douglas Cardinal, Canada

background: The Canadian Museum of Civilization, 1989.

left: The Canadian Museum of Civilization stands in a prominent position across the Ottawa River from Parliament in Hull, Quebec. Opened on June 29, 1989, on a 9.6-hectare (24-acre) site, the building is approximately 100,000 sq. m. (1,076,430 sq. ft) and comprises two distinct structures. The Glacier Wing is for public exhibitions, and the Canadian Shield Wing houses the Museum's main permanent collections, along with research laboratories and conservation and administration facilities.

left: The Glacier Wing reflects the Museum's symbolic depiction of the landscape at the end of the Ice Age, when humans first crossed into Canada. This ancient metaphor also comes through in the Manitoba limestone used as cladding, which contains fossils from the earliest epochs of the history of the land.

below: Characteristic of the Museum are the large walls of glass and the huge copper vaults and domes; there is more copper here than in any other building in the world.

conscious architecture

To understand the origins and purpose of life in its myriad forms and in its totality is an ancient human aspiration. It sustains our journey towards wholeness. It urges us to reach deep into ourselves, high above ourselves and into all things, so we can bear, celebrate and share the fruits of our journey.

The architect has a uniquely powerful medium in which to make this journey. When we enter the mystery of the creative process, the forms we make embody ourselves and bring into dynamic and living conversation what we were, what we are, and what we could be. The manner in which these forms flow out from us affirms our place in a wider world of community and nature. Our lives and architecture fuse as a continual metamorphosis of being and becoming: a journey of destruction and creation – a joyful dance between polarities and paradoxes; a way of transformation and understanding.

Much architecture rarely deals with more than style and momentary pre-occupations. However, like poetry, it can peel back the cultural layers, and with familiar elements create new meanings, create spaces and relationships which set up reverberations that can through time heal, delight, calm, awaken and move the soul. It can introduce the senses to the spirit, a gradual unfolding of the life-enhancing qualities inherent in the work – to plant a seed with a smile.

The 20th century saw a withering and severing of traditional values and reference points, and an inability to replace them with any deeply real alternatives. The world is in crisis on all levels, making it hard to keep our balance through rapid and often destructive changes. There are few constants. People have trouble finding purpose and meaning. Disorientation and alienation are common, especially in cities. Our society is sick, our earth home is sick. Our industrialized society has torn a rift between the sacred and the profane, and between nature and culture.

Gregory Burgess

The Brambuk Living Cultural Centre, Grampians National Park, Victoria, Australia, 1990. Designed and built with the Aboriginal community, this is a centre for the practice and teaching of indigenous culture. The timber pole frame is infilled with mudbricks, a central stone chimney supports plywood beams and colourbond steel roofing.

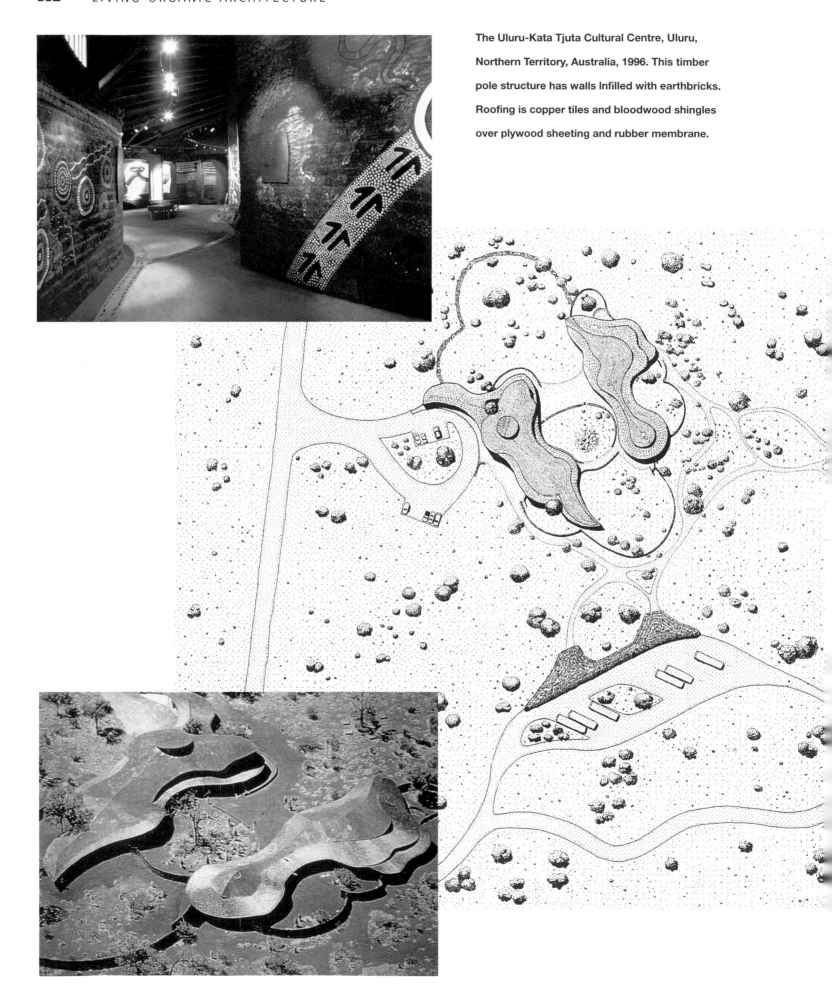

The Uluru-Kata Tjuta Cultural Centre, Uluru, Northern Territory, Australia, 1996. This timber pole structure has walls infilled with earthbricks. Roofing is copper tiles and bloodwood shingles over plywood sheeting and rubber membrane.

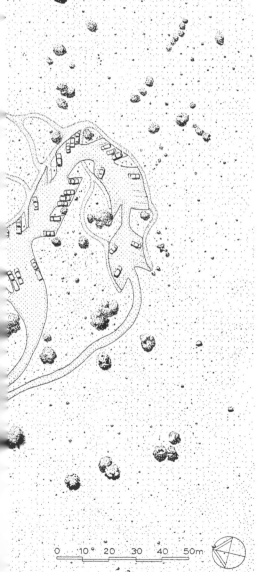

0   10   20   30   40   50m

With enthusiasm and humility we need to learn from the nature-integrated wisdom of what is left of the world's indigenous cultures (especially the Australian Aborigines). These cultures can remind us of many important things about life in community, nature and the cosmos. Their way has a roundness and a wholeness which stands in stark contrast to the manner in which our analytical and comparative thought processes have separated science, religion and art, so beginning the fragmentation of our post-enlightenment world.

We are struggling now to work creatively and communally with our individuality to awaken to the reality of one humanity and one earth and our shared responsibility for survival. It is a difficult and often painful journey. As an interpreter, facilitator and servant of the community, we bring our values into our work. These values matter.

In response to these challenges, we need to reintegrate feeling into our intelligence, and intelligence into our intuition so that our thoughts and actions are imbued with sympathy and wisdom, love and joy. Can we leave behind ego-centricity and self-expression and consecrate ourselves to the greater good, to that which gives meaning to the community and to the overall movement of civilisation? Architecture has great potential as a vehicle of exploration, and to be a catalyst for the awakening process. It can simultaneously offer us challenge, support, healing and inspiration as we continue our journey.

Gregory Burgess, Australia*

*extracts from *Thinking Architecture; Theory in the work of Australian Architects*, ed. Andrew Metcalf, 1995

roots and vision

I like to build in places
where nature is in the foreground
and cannot be overpowered by our temporary creations.
I use geometry not only to organize space and to mark
the social interactions within
but also to resonate with the landscape.

The building is not a fixed object
but part of the larger pattern that flows with change –
a permeable membrane responding to changes
in use and place.
I like to use natural materials
native to a place – earth, stone, reclaimed trees
together with the native intelligence of place
advanced technologies, scientific intelligence.

Architecture is part of the process of
"re-membering" – putting back together
our collective dreams.
The building should tell a story about place
and people – and be a pathway to understanding ourselves within nature.

S i m
V a n
d e r
R y n

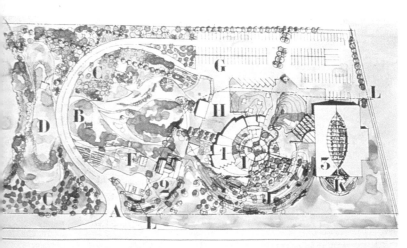

The Real Goods Solar Living Center, Hopland, California, 1996. Solar alignment is crucial to the Real Goods Center design, and the central courtyard acts as a solar calendar, with its central water spiral, living circle of trees, and the daily, weekly, and seasonal calendars. The upright poplars become a needle in a huge sundial, reflecting the sun's journey through the seasons.

What drives me is faith in the possibility of human culture and consciousness transcending a long obsession with objects and quantities and moving towards an ecological intelligence and compassion for everything that is alive.

I believe in cosmologist Arthur Young's notion that evolutionary processes follow a curve made of U-turns where the initial U-turn represents the leap from inanimate molecules to the first forms. I also subscribe to philosopher Jean Gebser's notion that humankind has evolved through four stages of culture/consciousness: the Magical, the Mythical and the Mental, and will inevitably evolve to the next stage which he calls the Integral – a state in which all earlier forms become accessible to us and are at the same time transcended by "integrality," a new form where we live in a state of connectedness and wholeness.

Mapping Gebser's structures of consciousness onto Young's diagram gives us the U-turn we now face. Either humanity makes the turn to an ecological world view and culture or we crash and burn as a civilization and perhaps as a species.

Perhaps that's too rigid for you. Sometimes it is for me too. The truth is that no one really knows what the future will bring. But I do know as a designer that when we approach the design of buildings and places by working with dynamic flows as well as static forms, when we think of the building as an organism as well as an object, when our clients become true partners rather than our masters or victims, then we have a real possibility of building an ecological present that increases our children's chances to create a liveable future.

Sim Van der Ryn, USA

In a few years time the red ochre soil cement and strawbale walls of the Real Goods showroom and store will be dwarfed by the height of the trees around the living fountain. Trees are the natural architecture of the courtyard, which will become a shady oasis as growth matures. In addition to the living poplar structure, an olive grove is plant-ed in the southwest quadrant of the courtyard, Texas umbrella trees provide individual shade spots, and vines are trained over the horizontal planes of the grape trellis, from which seats hang. Poplar-lined pathways provide more shady walkways leading into the centre of the space.

building – or digging deeper

Eric Furnémont

The mystery of our existence on the Earth is the deepest mystery of all. Underlying all our work is the need to question whatever we do as deeply as possible. Every architectural project is a project about life, an intuitive response to the questions that life poses, looking at a way of being at our specific time in history.

Ecology

Our decisions about building must come out of our consciousness of the planet if we do not want to be incriminated in its death. We must look to the wellbeing of the Earth itself and all who live here.

The Cahay-Lemoine residence, Liège, Belgium. Built predominantly of local brick, the exterior is partly clad in zinc. All the rooms flow out of one central passage, and all the interior decorating materials – paints, sealants, and varnishes – are organic.

Function and Form

To try and approach the essence of each space and its laws, architecture must take account both of the current needs of humanity and as yet unknown desires. It must create spaces which both embrace and confront us, demanding that we ask the relevant questions for life. What do we really need? What do we really want?

The economic and social process

How have humans seemed so able to forget the mystery upon which our physical existence is based? Instead people give priority to economic questions which are too often short term, with no respect for the life force that runs through everything. If architecture is a mirror of civilization, as shown in structures as diverse as our cathedrals, the nomad's desert tents and the square huts of the Dogons, what will be the image of our civilization in a thousand years if you imagine it seen through the innocent eyes of a newborn child?

We hope that our architecture will open ways to look at human questions, ways which refer us to our past to find solutions for the future. We cannot develop a new architecture which modifies our relationship with built space unless we radically alter traditional perceptions of those involved in construction. The building site is the place where this battle for change can be fought. But nothing will change unless architects have as their goal buildings that transform our perception of space with all its strengths and meanings.

Colour, Texture, and Scale

These are the three fundamental aspects of building and through these we make contact with the space. They are the real materials of our work. Add proportion, light, and shade, and a space will sing.

Unity and Diversity

Every project is a unique response to these questions. Every element of a project should be able to develop in its own appropriate way without ever forgetting the universal laws that govern it. Pulling together the pieces of the project into one clear unity without losing any of the character of the diverse parts – the very strength of architecture lies in this tension.

Paths to truth

Architecture is our legacy for humanity: we are not only building physical structures for our age but also memories for the future. We should be able to step back and move forward at the same time, combining strength with gentleness, rejecting both seductive short term ideas and ugliness. We must look at facts, materials, specific details with a new sense of wonder each time. We must build first and foremost for living, feeling human beings, never to make a statement about a particular style.

I try to build spaces which are imbued with a sense of divinity and timelessness, buildings which are overwhelmingly beautiful yet constructed with an overriding sense of reality. Joy and gratitude for being alive will always spring from those times and places where divine mystery and earthbound reality meet.

Eric Furnémont, Belgium

Barn at Aywaille, Belgium. The upper storey acts as a hay loft, the lower floor, which is part buried, is living accommodation. Below-ground walls are of stone, otherwise the building uses predominantly local larch wood for posts, beams, and shingles.

organic understanding

Daniel Liebermann

facing page: The Alexander residence (1990) illustrates the principles of accommodating a structure to its environment, taking full advantage of all the features of the landscape and the solar aspect. It nestles into a steep hillside near Berkeley, California.
above left: Flynn-McCone residence, 1989.
above right: Flynn-McCone residence, evaporative cooling tower, and pool aeration fount.
above centre: Tree-like central column roof of Menlo Park residence, 1978.
below: Point Reyes National Seashore Center for Ecological Habitats.

Woodbridge and other anthologies refer to my work as "influenced by Bruce Goff" and others. While Goff and Prince visited and camped at my studio in the early sixties, and Goff and Wright were indeed great mentors and inspirations, and guides into the future, my roots were laid earlier.

These earlier roots were severalfold, and laid a foundation for successive influences and actions: they include the Dutch colonial houses and barns of Essex, Morris, Monmouth counties of New Jersey where I grew up; the German and Dutch Colonial buildings of western New Jersey, the Delaware Watershed, and the virtual Carolingian social and building culture of the original Moravian and other religious communities.

Not far distant from Princeton, I could reach them by bicycle as a youth: their relationship to site, to sun, garden, grounded comfort, larger agronomy, general landscape of region surpassed all built efforts of successive generations. The earthy, egalitarian, communal, ethical, stable and economical also embodied the spiritual. Only the latter Taliesin experience approximated this lost late medieval way. Certainly Taliesin, embedded in both old Welsh rural life form and New England dissident ancient-modern social experimentation, was/is one of the few surviving geo-social erosional remnants of original American ideals and visions. (John Wright, Frank Lloyd Wright's father, was a New England Puritan/Unitarian radical pastor bearing the profound New England legacy... this influence is less attributed than the maternal side.)

Thoreau and Emerson and James *et al*, direct descendants of Old Boston and Harvard, are major figures in the formation of my early concepts of culture and meaning. With Thoreau the loop back wilfully to Nature is established. Inspiration has come from American Indian life ways, buildings, artefacts, including the earliest youth summer camps and emulations and studies of Indian ways in the North East of the USA, plus the ecology and economy of Indian constructs and existence. The birch bark canoe is a quintessential model of synergy, tensegrity, elegance and available grown resources; it was the beginning of my interest in environmental dynamic forces, here pure micro naval engineering. I have also been influenced by naval architecture at the scale of small sailing craft of the New England coast: wind, structure, shape: the critical and laminar relationships that make a working building.

By more expansive connection, Buckminster Fuller, the essential Yankee, above all signifies the deductive and rational discipline to derive pure eco-typical systems necessary for a future survivable human habitat of three dimensions (or more). Landscapes themselves influence, and the myriad and rich layering of these "built" environments layered up from rock, clay, running water and vegetation drainage, wind and solar exposure. All the influences, the in depth preoccupation with "constructs," with the moral dictat of Thoreau and Emerson and the Aborigine and Carolingian farmer, to the analytic vision of Stanley White (pioneer ecological landscape architect from Harvard), led to a solidification of a categorically imperative systemic view of a new world architecture one could call "Rational Organic Environmental Design," "Ecosystemic Architecture," or "International Rational Organic Architecture and Planning."

Subsequent influences were major: Ian McHarg and Paolo Soleri in their different ways, and today's (i.e. yesterday's) cutting edge pioneers such as Pliny Fiske, Wulf Hilberts, Sim van der Ryn. Finally the great organic structuralists, while often pure structuralists, have brought ecological structures from plant origins – the canoe, kayak, tepee, lodge, sailboat, clipper ship, barn – to the future forefront for a serious generation of new eco towns. Gaudí, Maillart, Candela, Otto and now Calatrava offer equally great and optimistic organic breakthroughs which will form the more integrated environments of the future.

These are the roots, forces, models and influences which have guided and formed my principle of design and my design. The integration of the many factors making a total human environment at the future communal level is a primary goal. I have tried to do this. The solidifying models, beyond the vestigial Carolingian towns of New Jersey and Pennsylvania, have been the surviving Shaker and Amish communities, Talicsin where I participated, Arcosanti which I have followed, and numerous intentional communities and ashrams, some of which such as Zendik Farm I have had a hand in physically designing.

Over two decades ago I composed a large monograph of my ideas and works entitled *The Horizontal Cathedral*. This curious title was intended to provoke thought and curiosity, meant to create an under template for the future, in which faith, spirituality, feeling, reverence and stewardship of life and world were dominant. But in the new community the differentiated exercises of religion *per se* and communal lay-life would become integrated, cross-pollinated, much as in the Carolingian *avant-garde* Monastic "City." Reverence for all manner of earthly conduct, as well as responsible and creative doing of it would largely be the "religion." This is the challenge facing modern civilization: a concerted effort to plow in all recent climactic urban

top: Solarium House extension, 1998.
above: Constructing the Center for
Ecological Habitats at Point Reyes
National Seashore, several small
clustered and free structures.

left: Central structural paraboloid column
at Flynn McCone residence, San Rafael,
California, 1989. Buildings predicated
upon minimum land use, minimal disturbance, and maximum site sensitivity
often feature a central tree-like column
and radiating roof framing to accommodate elliptical floor plans and maximum
solar orientation and earthquake
resistance.

below: staircase at the Alexander residence, Berkeley, 1990.

modalities of "civilization" and reform these to a more humane, gratifying, sustainable-economical and disciplined way is becoming an imperative for physical and spiritual survival. A new city model can be inspiring, brilliant, functional, gratifying: models are necessary now; they can and should spring up anywhere and everywhere, and at a small working scale no larger than Taliesin, Arcosanti or Shrewsbury. The tools and talent are mustering, wonderful new beginnings can happen.

In my own specific small architecture the virtual technology is a function of economic-limits-reality. Much material is recycled. Almost all of my structures are solar, land shape (topo), earthquake and earth-stability grounded; they are often based in steep hillsides typical of coastal California; they are all predicated upon a minimum land-site displacement or disturbance and reconstruction. As a result most are tree-like, with central steel, concrete or timber trunk-like columns and fan-like radiating roof framing to accommodate odd long elliptical floor plans. The rude derivation of most of my floor plans begins not with an *a priori* housing concept of tradition, but rather an immediate and direct sensitivity to the site itself, given factors of sun exposure, north side protection, forest fire, wind heat loss and fire spread, heat containment via earth, sod, thermopane, etc., and ground insulation.

All these numerous small dwelling complexes are comprised of very small habitat units, family nests. Pine II, the earliest paradigmatic model in Mill Valley, California, is only 850 sq. ft (79 sq. m) and quite an adequate environment in which to raise a family of parents and children. The new Center for Ecological Habitats at Point Reyes National Seashore is composed of several clustered and free structures, the largest of which is under 2,000 sq. ft (186 sq. m) and the smallest under 200 sq. ft (19 sq. m).

What rules these environments is the deep interrelationship with site, landscape, gardening, weather control, and use, least site disturbance, direct shaping by existing land contour, sun and wind. Finally, arising from these rules and controls a most subtle and important by-product has emerged by itself, and this is perhaps one of the most promising, effortless, and powerful tools

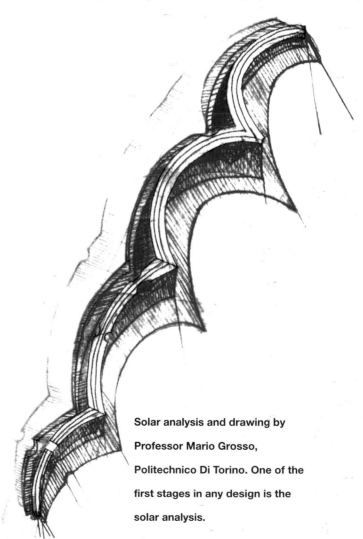

Solar analysis and drawing by Professor Mario Grosso, Politechnico Di Torino. One of the first stages in any design is the solar analysis.

of the future: that is a rule or law of perception itself. By the sheer bending of small buildings to accommodate the hillside form, by the creation of small buildings which are relatively open, born by central tree-like columns, and curvilinear and cupped dam-like three dimensional solar reflecting, and insulating walls, the depth of the phenomenon of perception itself has appeared. Most persons visiting, dwelling or working in these buildings observe or feel a sense of space, size and magnitude far greater than the nominal known size of the dry language of measurements. Indeed these spaces cannot be defined by square feet, the walls can contribute endless vistas, and contain their own three dimensions such as a wind filled ship's sail. Often only two long walls define, not four.

This new world of sensitive and observant consciousness of space and human perception, and the profound interrelationship of the two, may be one of the most important aspects of the coming "wave" of organic architecture. The economies implicit are enormous. The direct human gratification of spatial perceived needs, if understood more deeply, can reduce the size of built human habitations vastly, mitigating future impact, destruction, and cost of construction and operation. And of course a truer understanding of how we see, with our mind and eye, is the foundation of everything organic. Man's eye and brain evolved over aeons of time, most of which were within the vast untrammelled and unpaved landscape of our Edenic biosphere. We must go to Nature for our models now, that is clear!

Dan Liebermann, USA

top: Pine II car deck.

above: Pine II, the earliest model for a small space economical environmental dwelling, the Liebermann Payne Studio, Mill Valley, California, 1961.

left: The main living space of the Alexander residence continues to reflect the influence of the landscape through natural materials, sloping and curving surfaces, and open spaces. In this steep southwest exposed hillside the high strength reinforced concrete walls serve as the main retaining and foundation structure. Key features include solar collectors and radiators, finished interior enclosures and surfaces, earthquake stabilizers, reflected sunlight sources. The comparatively small floor areas appear far greater than their abstract measurements.

Everything is interrelated

Balkrishna Doshi

Everything is interrelated. From the design of a pin to a design of a metropolis. All that one needs to understand is the differences in the scales and their spheres of impact. And even though each object, issue and design should have its own identity, it cannot be conceived in isolation since identity is a mere comparison with what is immediately around and very often this perception is short sighted.

In architecture I firmly believe that the final design of any building must rise beyond mundane needs and towards the subtle contexts, the contexts of being alive. In my projects I want to express my journey in search of the "soul" of an architecture which would be valid for ever. A building must not only be built well, it should also be able to put down roots and should contain sufficient experiences to communicate and survive for many generations to come.

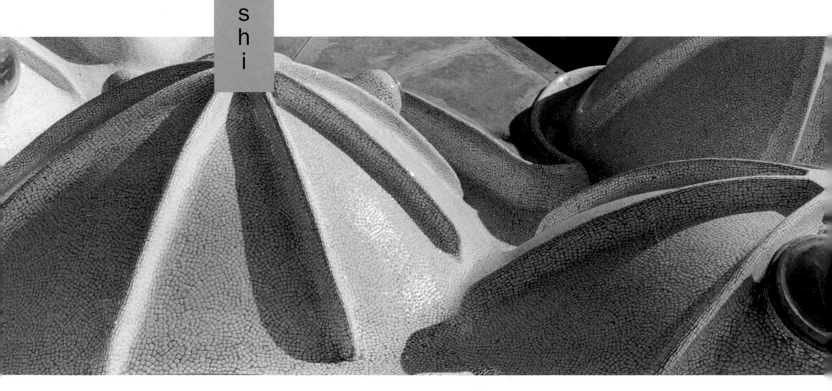

The domed roofs and curving walls of the interior gallery space of the Hussain-Doshi Gufa in Ahmedabad.

Constructed of thin ferrocement shells without any form work, the Hussain-Doshi Gufa is based on a model of intersecting circles and ellipses, but its inclined domes, curvilinear walls, undulating floors, and non-rectilinear columns relieve any centredness suggested by the plan. A footprint of 280 sq. m. (3,000 sq. ft) nearly doubles its surface area through convoluting planes. Buried spaces, earth mounds, raised volumes, and mosaic finish make the building energy conscious in a hot dry climate.

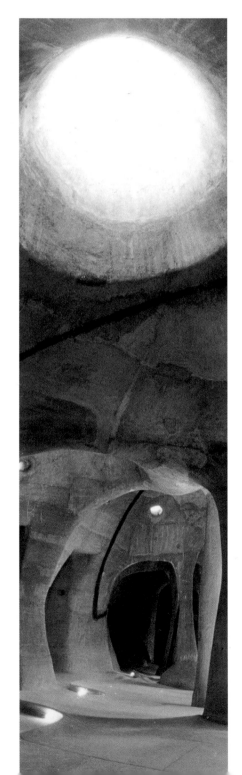

All choices of technologies or materials or functions should be born out of their own nature and needs. Their own evolution gives them a character and demonstrates to us their purpose or use. Hence what we need to do is to allow the purpose of existence to find its relatedness or application.

Form should not be finite but should be amorphous so that the experience within is loose, meandering and multiple. Space is not merely an open or an enclosed area, but it also has a mythical sense, a sense which touches the inner perception of what it should be. Each individual, each community has its own preferences, and they should be allowed to express themselves symbolically. Absorption of symbolic nuances should be encouraged and appropriate aesthetic values should be adopted in architectural design. Buildings are meant for people – and this includes literate, illiterate, young and old – and there must be a dialogue between buildings and their users.

All planning should be open-ended and capable of spatial adjustments for we must recognise that "time" is not in our hands and changes do take place over years. Like style, time is a limited notion that can be easily set aside if we realise that all that we are presently perceiving is seen through our memories of past and present, and that there are layers which must be seen together and not as fragmented issues be they of art, architecture or life. Whenever we build, it is essential that we look from a distance with eternity or timelessness as our basis so that our solutions are holistic and enduring.

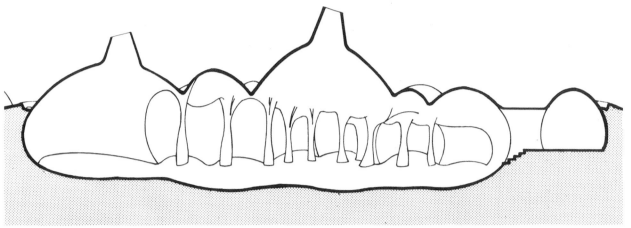

left and below: Tejal's house, Vadodara, 1997. Apertures in the free-form ferro-cement roof structure and in the walls allow for the kinetic play of sunlight and shadow patterns on the interior and outside surfaces.

"All these years have been a long and rather unusual journey. The drops which coalesced at the source gradually became a spring, then a river and now a part of many rivers. In the process of this journey, many lands were traversed, some open and some controlled. There were moments when the flow ebbed, even stopped, but the stagnation gave rise to a lake. Then the floods overpowered the embankments and pulled me out of the slumber.

The journey saw many lands, forests and gardens over many seasons. In the process the river drank the water sanctified by great visionaries and the water began to raise questions. The muddy waters began to clear and the journey finally found its path. Though still not clear, there is a path which pulls strongly from deep within, hearing the silent waves of the ocean. It appears that the vast ocean has much to say to the river and the drops which have travelled far."

Balkrishna Doshi, India

below and right: Sangath, the architect's office, and
headquarters of the Vastu-Shilpa Foundation,
Ahmedabad, is a complex where activities related to
architecture, planning, and crafts are encouraged.
Sangath is designed with different structural systems,
varying levels and rhythms, light from different sources,
and varied shapes and surfaces so the building
constantly evokes surprise and encourages people to
explore, gathering the information they need at certain
points of time and space.

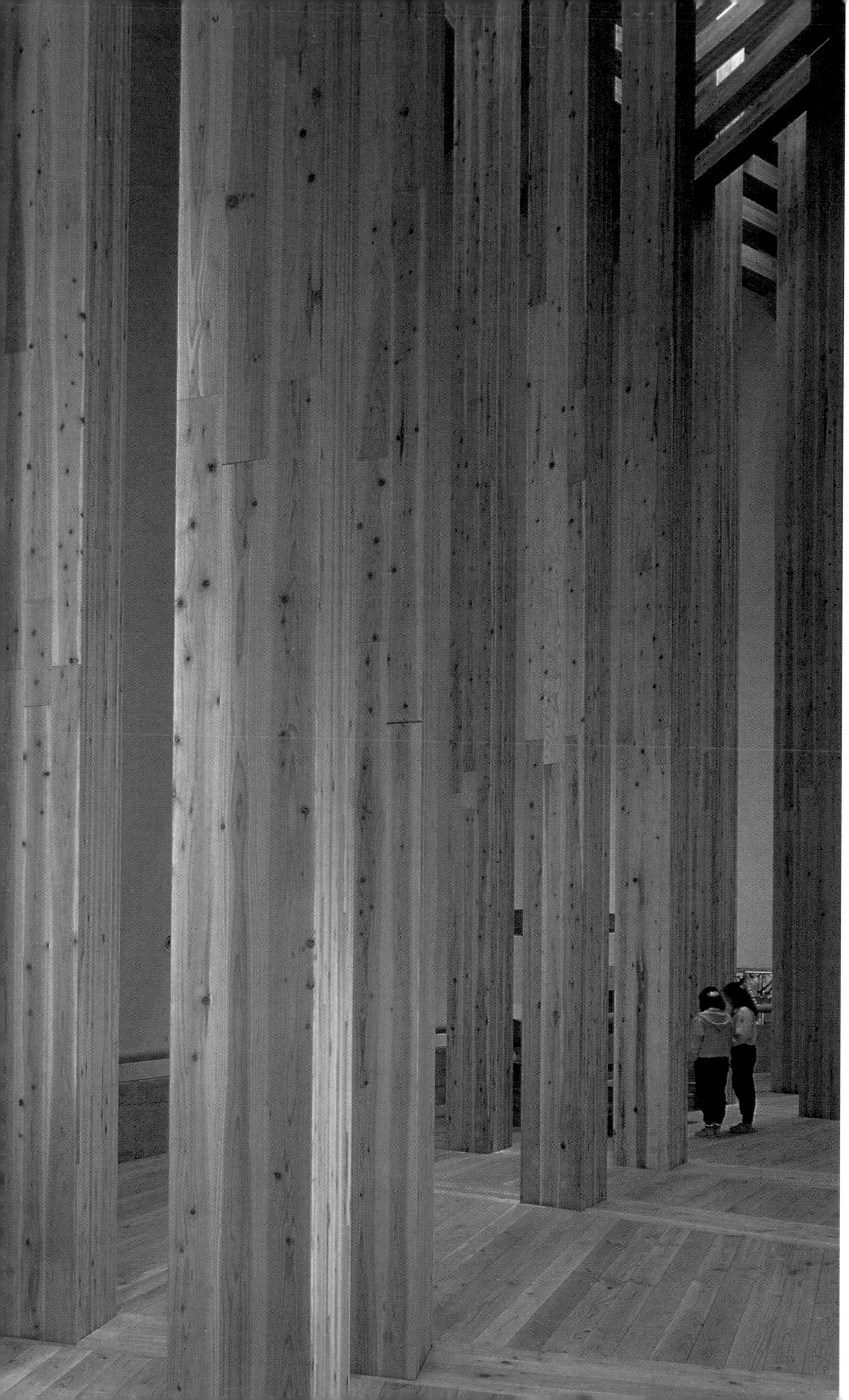

Tadao Ando

wood culture

In these times of apprehension over the crisis of our earthly environment and the deterioration of our spiritual culture, it is important that we seek a new beginning – through new understandings of our environment and in a new appreciation of forests and the culture of wood, for these can bring richness to the heart of man.

The Museum of Wood at Mikata-gun, Hyogo, was built to celebrate 45th National Tree Day. It is situated in a region enjoying rich strands of forest, an area blessed with a unique natural environment due to its location, close to the Pacific Ocean, and the culture that environment has produced.

The first consideration of this project was to avoid cutting the existing forest, wherever possible. The Museum, it was felt, should grow naturally in its site within the enclosing trees.

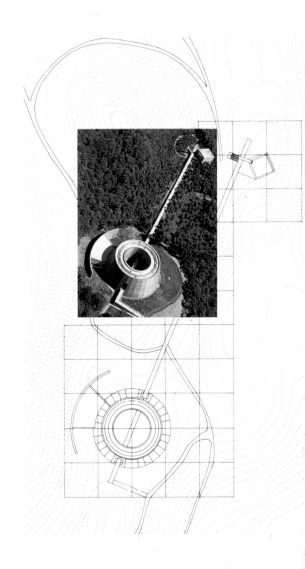

The Museum plan is ring shaped – 46 m (150 ft) in diameter – and contains a one room round space, 18 m (60 ft) high. Pillars stand aligned on a circular arc within this space, which displays the characteristic power of space formed by wooden pillar and beam construction. Here, items relating to the cultures of forests and wood are exhibited, along a curvilinear ramp winding right through the centre of the ring. The space in the centre of the building which is devoted to a pond – provides a dramatic meeting point of sky and water. A sloping bridge penetrates the building, crossing the pond and leading to the annexe, which proffers views of a rich enclosure of forest.

Visitors to the Museum experience both the profound wealth of the deep forest, and – in the powerful space produced by the building – a recreating of the human culture that is nourished by that wealth. Then they are released into the space between pure sky and water. In this way, the Museum affords real experience of the profound relationship uniting human culture with nature.

Tadao Ando, Japan

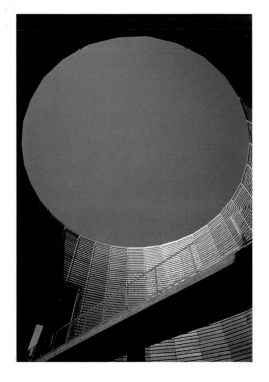

Museum of Wood, Mikata–gun, Hyogo, Japan, 1994.

Drew and James Hubbell

thoughts on how I build –

"Four walls
a prison makes
but if within
a flower grows
four walls
a garden makes."

My life as an artist began when I was in my teens, with a love affair for horses and nature. At that time I began painting and drawing horses, eventually getting into sculpture. Then, because of building our own home, I became involved in architecture.

For me, art and architecture have always been a search for self-understanding. My approach to design is much like a courtship where I must respect all the aspects of the building that is trying to come into form and include them in what the building will become.

The first building I constructed was very much tied to the earth. It was an anchor for my life. Now when I think about building, I still want it committed to the earth but open and accepting of the entire universe.

I do not believe there should be one way of doing buildings. Each building has its own way to be. It is the architect's job to listen to the process. Buildings should try to heal the scepticism we find around us.

The words I would place high in the design process are respect, beauty and trust.

Located on a hill overlooking the Pacific Ocean, the semicircular Guest House at La Jolla, California, was built in 1990, designed as a retreat and place for healing. The guest house has numerous intricate details, including stained-glass clerestories (below) that reflect on the interior ceilings at night, an exterior mosaic fountain, a mosaic shower, and carved wood and stained-glass doors.

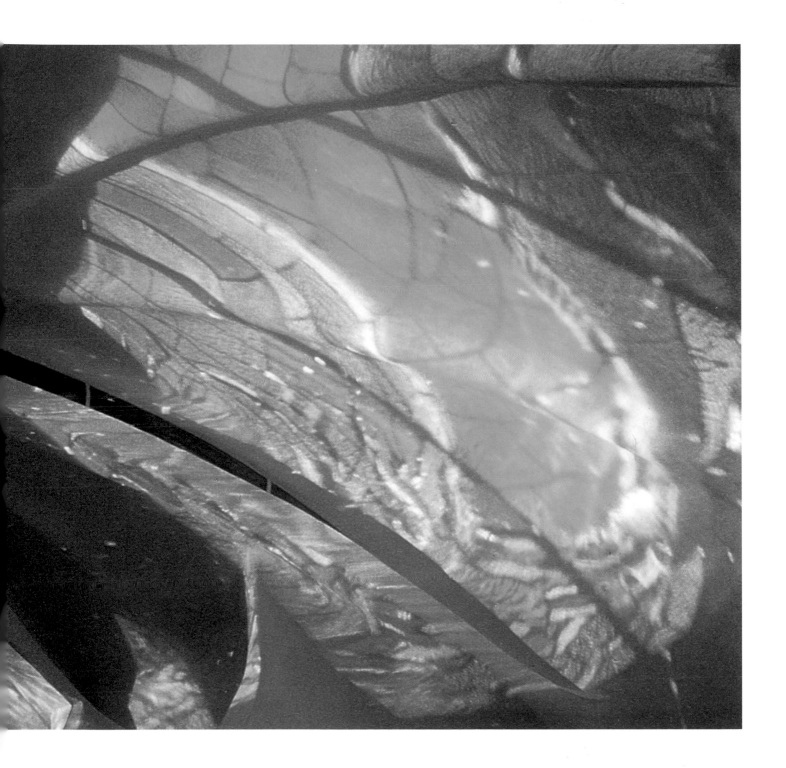

BUILDING A BRIDGE FROM CLAY TO JOIN THE STARS

Out of clay, from stardust, we are made. We have arrived here at a time that hearkens back to the Gothic, where the world was whole, not sorted and boxed, where understanding also came from the heart, and where the unknown gave meaning to what we thought we knew.

Is it the job of arts and architecture to embrace all of life? All that it means to be human in a world of 60 billion galaxies as well as wind in a spider's web? Can architecture embrace a world as complex as we have made it? Can it celebrate the shadows and light within us?

Nature is embedded in us down to our toenails; the earth is where we come from and where we go. Stardust is measured in our molecules. We may be flickering candles, afloat in an eternity of time and space. Can we, these specks of dust, coming from the mud, sing to the stars?

Can the human heart form such a world? Can architecture and the arts help to find a world of meaning, grace and beauty?

James Hubbell, USA

above: West entry to the Kuchumaa Eco Center, Tecate, Mexico, 1998. Designed in collaboration with Arquitectura Solar, this complex consists of a classroom, workshop/office, and a theatre. Buildings fit into the surrounding landscape, with patios and work areas to create outdoor rooms. They use natural lighting, passive cooling and heating, and thin-shell concrete construction.

far left: Carved wood door and stained glass at the Center.

left: Stained-glass window in dome classroom.

right: Resin model of Deep Dream Underwater House, a retreat and metaphor of a return to the place where life began. Designed for a site 30 m. (95 ft) beneath the ocean, near La Jolla, California, 1995.

soul roots

Vitor Ruivo Forte

We must always keep looking at our work and ways of working, inspired and pushed forward by joy and passion. A work does not have a beginning or an end. It is a constant, something that lives within us, searching and waiting for opportunities to express itself. It is a process of looking both inside and out-side ourselves that continues unceasingly and regularly just like a pendulum.

Space is an abstract entity. It cannot be defined and characterized by sur-faces or areas. In order for space to be transformed into a living vibrating body or sustainable edifice it must be given expression through rhythm, force, and dynamism, and it must be gifted with light which will then constitute its soul

The act of creating is quite different from simply describing. Creation is an activity that involves the soul and cannot be sepa-rated from it. It is not a matter of working with material things in search of soul, but every creative action is informed by simultane-ous soul activity, the two go hand-in-hand. The act of creation produces the forms, shapes, rhythms and concepts that speak to different parts of us and fill many spaces in ourselves.

The root of any building is the metamorphosis of light, it is through that process, the transformation of the light in our soul, that abstract spaces can become solid buildings.

Vitor Ruivo Forte, Portugal

facing page: Interior detail below ground at the Hotel Casa Blanca, Porto.
facing page (inset): Entrance to the restored and extended Monastery at Balsamaõ, North Portugal.
right: Staircase tower at Balsamaõ Monastery.

culture and architecture

Renzo Piano

When we say "culture" we usually mean our own: a fine soup blended from Leonardo da Vinci and Freud, Kant and Darwin, Louis XIV and Don Quixote. In the Pacific it is not just the recipe that is different but the ingredients as well. We can approach their soup with detachment, bringing our own cutlery. Or we can try to understand how it was born, why it has gone in certain directions, what philosophy of life has shaped it. I didn't bring my own cutlery to New Caledonia, all I brought were my skills and those of the Building Workshop: the techniques needed to create spaces and construct buildings. My proposal had made the effort to be born there, thinking Kanak. Working in

the Antipodes, with a people whose existence was almost unknown to me just a few months earlier, was a wonderful challenge. Moreover it was not just a tourist village that I had to build. I had to create a Symbol: a cultural centre devoted to Kanak civilization, the place that would represent them to foreigners and that would pass on their memory to their grandchildren. Nothing could have been more loaded with symbolic expectations.

The spirit of the Pacific is ephemeral, and the constructions of the Kanak tradition are no exception. They are born out of unity with nature, using the perishable materials it provides. The continuity of the village in time is not

this page and overleaf: The Kanak cultural centre stands on a promontory to the east of Nouméa, in a natural setting of great beauty. The expression of an age-old tradition of harmony with nature, the centre is not and could not be enclosed within a monumental structure. It is not a single building but an assemblage of villages and open spaces planted with trees, of functions and routes, of solids and voids.

based on the duration of the individual building but on the preservation of a topology and pattern of construction. When drawing up the project, we worked on both lanes. We sought a strong link with the territory, which would embed the centre in the geography of the island. From local culture we stole the dynamic elements, the tension that would serve to bind the construction to the life of the inhabitants.

The huts are the dominant and unifying element of the project. There are ten, of three different sizes, from fairly small to a scale that matches the surrounding tall trees. The largest forms a clearly visible landmark at 28 m (92 ft) tall. These constructions are an expression of the harmonious relationship with the environment that is typical of Kanak culture. The link is not just aesthetic, but also functional, exploiting the characteristics of the New Caledonian climate – the cases are equipped with a very efficient system of passive ventilation, the air circulating freely between the cladding of the external bowed and the interior vertical skin. The system also gives the cases a "voice". Together they make a distinctive noise, the sound of the Kanak villages and their forests.

Accepting the challenge inherent in the programme meant taking off the mental clothes of the European architect and steeping myself in the world of the people of the Pacific. The project, carried out in collaboration with Paul Vincent, was the most reckless of my many ventures into other fields. The dread of falling into the trap of a folkloric imitation, of straying into the realm of kitsch and picturesque, was a constant worry.

Throughout the process I received a great deal of support and understanding: the people of the island saw the cases as a sincere attempt to enter into the spirit of the Pacific Ocean and to pay a tribute to the local civilisation. The Kanaks have helped me to improve the project.

It must be said that, quite apart from good intentions and respect due other cultures, a proposal based on our own models would simply not have worked in New Caledonia. It was not possible to offer a standard product of Western architecture, with a layer of camouflage over the top: it would have looked like an armoured car covered with plain leaves. A mistaken concept of universality could have led me to apply my mental categories of history and progress outside the context in which they developed, a grave error.

True universality in architecture can be attained only through connection with the roots, gratitude for the past, and respect for the *genius loci*.

Renzo Piano, Italy*

* from *Renzo Piano Logbook*, Thames and Hudson, London, 1997

below and facing page: The sculptural Truss Wall house in Tokyo was created by bending reinforcing bars into shape and covering them in wire mesh into which wet concrete was poured. This allowed for fluid integration of different independent shapes. The sense of movement continues through the interior spaces and fittings as well as the external form.

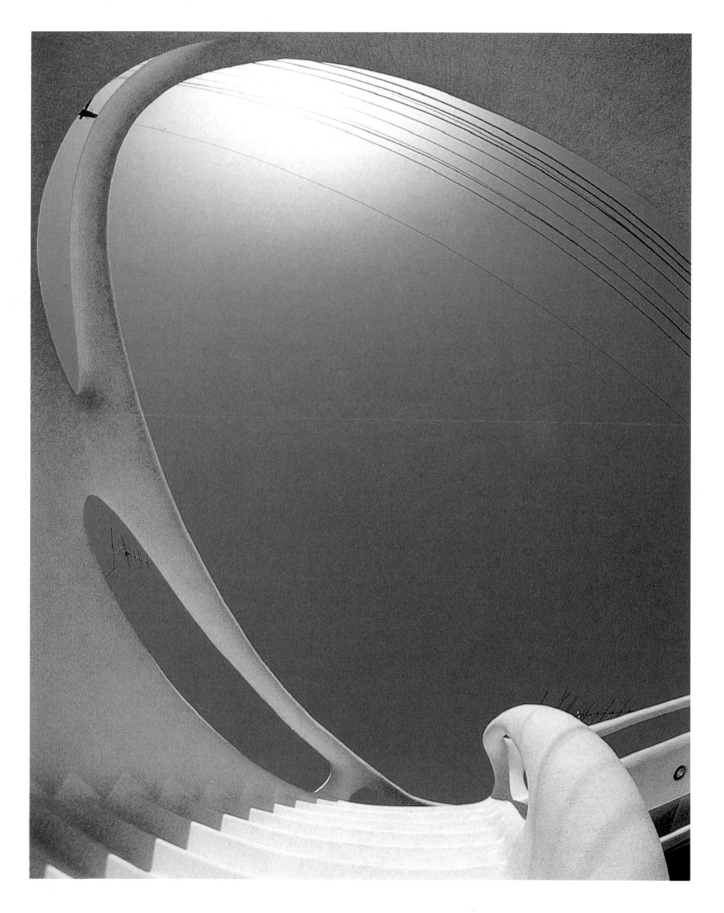

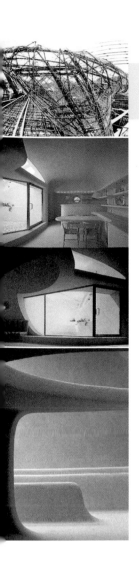

Eisaku Ushida and Kathryn Findlay

parallel landscapes

We are a bicultural partnership, Japanese and British. This means we are simultaneously familiar and unfamiliar with the things around us. This duality forms the basis of our work. Having lived in two different cultures seems to have given us an objective and critical perspective towards the conventions in society.

The definitions of architecture are becoming increasingly ambiguous. The modes of composition and social systems which supported past notions of architecture are no longer able to meet the demands of a rapidly changing society. The conditions surrounding urban architecture are having a particularly subversive effect on the concept of architecture. Yet builders, designers and clients alike continue to produce and procure increasingly uninspired and oppressive living environments which are little more than assemblages of industrial products and stock response design. A variety of social factors contribute to this, but perhaps the most fundamental is a certain self limiting attitude that plagues us all as individuals.

The global trend towards a borderless society, culture, and technology has produced a pressing need to urgently rethink how we all inhabit our shared environment, free of national and disciplinary restrictive practices. In order to assist this process, as architects we must fundamentally re-evaluate our received notions of what architecture is and evolve an open-ended system which incorporates rather than divides the various disciplines so that architecture, landscape and sculpture may all inform each other towards a wider view of spatiality.

In Japan the individual has become the basic social unit. The family has not been totally negated but the emphasis is on a community no longer based on territorial/blood relations but on the will of the individual. Communications are no longer conducted exclusively in physical but also in electronic space. In this context spaces must be created to accommodate the innumerable encounters of freely moving persons who drift throughout the city; and the city itself must be programmed as a vessel to contain this Brownian movement. Residential and urban space in Japan have begun to meld into one another.

Contemporary Japanese cities have developed unique strategies for overcoming their cramped conditions. The domestic functions of eating, bathing, sleeping have begun to proliferate within the city – in comfortable cafés, relaxed bars and karaoke boxes, counter eateries and fast food stops, spa clubs, saunas, love hotels, hostess bars... This kind of social fluctuation has an influence at the individual level of the residence. On one hand individual space is being capsulised and miniaturised, while on the other, semi-public space such as the living room or kitchen is becoming tied to the city. Two aspects of dwelling are moving simultaneously in opposite directions.

Human beings make no attempt to see things which they cannot comprehend. Until the discovery of Chaos theory, chaos just appeared to be non coherent. Ever since advances in computer technology made it possible for Mandelbrot and Julia to render visible their ideas of chaos geometry we have begun to realise the potential of new geometry.

Architecture is founded on natural and social topography. Large scale urban development has robbed us of an awareness of how people in the past understood their relationship to the land. We are not however simply suggesting a return to tradition, rather we propose correcting the errors created by lack of forethought in the past through this kind of diachronic perspective – by re-assessment of the relationship of man to his terrain.

The Situationists explored the effects of the geography of the twentieth century city on the emotions and behaviour of its citizens. They evolved a philosophy of the city and found meaning in the physical and psychological patterns of the city street. They found that in each area in the city the inhabitants have their own invisible and mental map. Other commentators advocate that we maintain an open-ended intellectual stance towards a wide range of possibilities.

In urban Japan we find that rigidly held received notions about land-use, topography and architecture have created a blinkered view of the city and limited awareness of its potential. An oppressive urbanism is the result. We subscribe to the view that in the employment of artistic processes in the city we can bring into play a creative and vital interpretation of the city which is able to empower its inhabitants and to refashion the environment.

Exposing the potential in a situation as progressive agent can cultivate a spirit of continuity with the "other", and can be a positive force which counteracts the simple delineation of borders. This is surely the only way out of the current deadlock in contemporary Japan.

Eisaku Ushida and Kathryn Findlay, Japan

Inspired by Salvador Dali's statements on future architecture, the Soft and Hairy House in Ibaraki, Japan, is an expression of surrealism among conventional housing. The original green landscape of the site was transferred to the house's roof. The blue egg shaped bathroom is in an extruded concrete bubble in the courtyard, the tactile interior includes walls swathed in canvas and a door wrapped in fake fur.

seeds of inspiration

I was born in Joplin, Missouri and lived there for the first eighteen years of my life. Throughout that time I developed a love of nature, from "spelunking" the caves and mines of the area to studying the moss-covered log habitats of creatures that lived within. At eighteen I went to Georgia Technical College to become an aeronautical engineer because I love the lightness of flight.

Soon after arriving at college, some intuitive force hit me with the revelation of architecture, leading me into this life. I soon transferred to Norman, Oklahoma, to study with Bruce Goff, who encouraged me to be myself, no matter what. This meant combining my love of nature with the lightness of flight and the traits and wishes of clients into one grand mixture. I spent most of my early life as an architect with few clients, but I had precious time to let ideas naturally form into organic being.

above left: Hawthorne Art Gallery, Big Sur, California, 1997, houses

works by five artists of the same family.

above: Scharffenberger residence, Big Sur, California, 1999. The

wooden roof structure echoes the shape of an ocean wave.

The Muennig house, Big Sur, California, 1997.

main picture right: A waterfall cools the house in
the hot summer weather.

inset top right: Exterior sod roof.

inset centre right: Interior radiating roof beams.

When I met Bruce Goff at the University of Oklahoma he was teaching a course called Architecture 273 which consisted of music described in architectural terms – he gave lectures on rhythm using examples from Stravinsky and then he described the difference between rhythm and cadence. Cadence was the repetition of a beat (1,2,1,2 etc) but Stravinsky had rhythm which was a whole composition of music moving toward completion. And then he gave us projects to design expressing rhythm, reflection, counterpoint, articulation and many of the different elements of musical composition. Every Thursday night the students met for music sessions at Goff's house where he played contemporary classical music. He turned off the lights and had everybody lie on the floor so they could not be distracted from the music. He also had exhibits of Japanese prints and fairytale illustrations by Kay Neilson, Edmond Dulac and others on the walls so that students could gain inspiration for their drawings.

I worked with him for two summers before, and for a short time after I graduated. He always, after a day's work, either played a piece of music or went to his rare book collection and showed us how a particular book had influenced him. We went to New York together and along the way visited a Walter Burleigh Griffin House in St Louis, Missouri and Frank Lloyd Wright's Dana House in Springfield, Illinois, his Robie House at the University of Chicago and many of his houses in the Oak Park area. We also visited several Sullivan banks. We also spent an evening in New York with the composer Edgar Varèse. These experiences had a big influence on me.

After graduating from Oklahoma, I spent several years studying as an apprentice, before eventually returning to Joplin, Missouri, to build the Foulke House. This was inspired by a burnt down grinding mill, with water wheel, which had been a local landmark on the site. The house was built of pieces of timber 18 ft (5.5 m) long and 2 x 6 in (50 x 150 mm) thick, which formed a wooden shell structure which was reminiscent of the rolling water wheel. It felt good to do something timeless with one foot in the past in the imagery of the water wheel and the other in the future with the implications of the structure.

Herb Greene was also an influence on me as a teacher in school and after. He continued my education on the importance of imagery in architecture, suggesting that architecture is indeed tied together through imagery, a notion that is no longer held important. We went together to the World Fair in Montreal 1967 where I was particularly impressed by Habitat, the Czechoslovakian, Canadian, and Frei Otto's German pavilions.

In 1971 I took a vacation to Big Sur, California, which I immediately accepted as home. I moved there and built a 16 ft (5 m) diameter glass tepee to live in for a year while I built my main house. Eighteen years later I moved into the main house.

Building in Big Sur has its challenges. Monterey County laws prohibit building on a hillside that slopes more than 30 per cent, nor can a house silhouette on a ridge. Houses may not be visible from the scenic coastal Highway 1. Many building sites are a 45 minute drive up a dirt road that may be impassable in rainy times. Electricity has not been brought to the location of many houses. This is a remote area, wild in its dramatic extremes: drought, flood, forest fire, earthquakes, the one highway washing away in winter storms that can cut the area off for months at a time. But it is also spectacularly beautiful. From these conditions I have defined my palette of materials: concrete for fire resistance, durability, heat mass, plasticity,

left: The McDade residence, Big Sur, California, 1999, has an indoor/outdoor hot tub in a garden room. Laminated beams set at 30° off vertical form a structure curving in two directions.

right: The Paul Witt guest house incorporates curved, laminated beams that reflect the surrounding hills and ocean.

earthquake resistance; redwood for its resistance to moisture and rich color; high tech glass for its low heat transfer and transparency.

I have tried over the years to let each house express one main idea. The Foulke House expresses the character of the flowing river and the rolling water wheel. The Scharfenberger House expresses an ocean wave. The McDade House expresses the two distinct views, the view of the oak trees from the bedroom and the distant ocean view from the living room. The Witt Caretaker House curves with its unique mountain site. The Hawthorne Gallery expresses the art that it contains. My house expresses its cavernous qualities.

When I create a house based on the organic tradition I find it is always alive, and a living tribute to the people for whom it was created.

Mickey Muennig, USA

P
e
t
e
r

H
ü
b
n
e
r

the built relationship

House is, in its form and material, without genetic definition. There doesn't seem to be anything like an "original house", which is why humans have been able to settle anywhere on earth. However, this ability to adapt has to cope with constraints and the nature of evolutionary biology: people need their own territory. A house must offer protection and comfort, peace and security, but it must also be a place of communication and interaction, allowing for intimacy and stimulation. We should have a physical relationship with our home but also, more importantly, a symbolic relationship on an emotional level.

A house should have a recognisable form and function, but individualistic design and specifications are important, and a connection with plants and nature should be aimed for. A house must maintain the inhabitants' health and well-being, and must not constrain their mobility. So the house is not primarily a material-physical structure but it is also a psychological-cognitive object. The result of the elemental need to be housed fulfils essential biological functions.

Humans are much closer to buildings than is commonly thought. Buildings are, in a way, our 'third skin'. Now that our skin is no longer in direct contact with our surroundings but is instead protected from the elements by clothing and houses, we begin to understand that our buildings must adhere to certain rules that satisfy more than just aesthetic demands. Active exchange with our surroundings helps focus and stimulate our senses.

When the eventual users or inhabitants-to-be are included in the process of planning and construction, it is possible to build truly creative yet functional and elemental buildings. We must shape our built environment according to our needs – not the other way round.

above: Interior roof of the Waldorf School kindergarten at Kircheim unter Teck, Germany.

left: Even the youngest students help with the construction of their building.

far left: Roof constructed from a web of 24 beams, built with the students.

below: Wooden shingles represent the scales and rough hewn pillars become the limbs of the dinosaur at the café at the Stammheim Youth Centre

right: Entrance to the café.

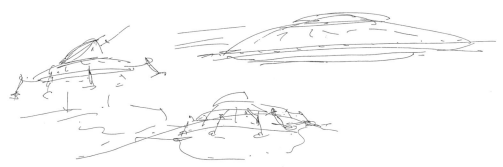

below: The Youth Centre building at Glingen links cosmic and earthbound realities, resembling a spacecraft that has recently settled on the ground.

Over the last few years we have been involved in many self-build projects with hundreds of young people and this experience has made us realise the strength of the desire for people to build their own shelter, what enormous potential young people have to shape their surroundings, and how big their creative energy is as long as we allow them, under careful guidance, to house themselves.

Building with people for people is a rewarding adventure, and a good house is the reward for the intense and long process of communal effort. Future generations may judge if this is a viable way of creating good architecture. Apparently young home builders are simply following their innate, original abilities. In their naivety they are able to create beautiful spaces which are affectionately used and passionately looked after. Building then becomes a psycho-social process, the products of which are houses of a unique quality; they can tell their own stories, originating from the heads, hearts and hands of so many. Even during their construction process, these houses experience strong emotional affection, which makes them become richer and richer when they are lived in.

Peter Hübner, Germany

Shoei Yoh

phenomenological architecture

My liberation from the ancient geometrical approach of architecture began in 1990 when I was designing the Totyama Galaxy Gymnasium to support heavy snow loading. Instead of increasing the depth of the flat roof truss, I experimented with deforming the structure via computer simulation to find the optimum shape. Surprisingly, this automatic deformation made by the snow resulted in an unusual and irregular form. The optimum form was natural, rational and economical. It minimized the volume of steel used, thereby reducing CO_2 and making a more sustainable community design. It was just the beginning of Phenomenological Architecture, which can give a form that looks like a cloud in the sky or a galaxy in the universe. These ideas were further developed in the Odawara Sports Complex and the Glass Station where discontinuity between part and whole, external forces and internal requirements gave a complex and compliant character to the smooth fluidity of the buildings.

In the Naiju Community Center community participation and the use of local materials were basic conditions. We looked for an interaction with nature through layering intuitively-conceived forms and natural forms in the environment. Finally we used bamboo to develop a square tensile structure, stiffened by folding, and anchored to the ground. This was temporarily supported by a central post. The bamboo lattice was then covered with wet concrete poured non-stop for several days. After three weeks this set to make a compressive shell dome, allowing the central post to be removed. This free form of a giant square folded bamboo handkerchief is another example of natural phenomena responding to nature. Local craftsmen and community members helped to assemble the bamboo shell, and in order to bend and deflect the bamboo into shape, they lit a great bonfire inside! This was the only method we could think of. The result was a feeling of joint ownership and collaborative effort that none of those involved had imagined. The folds in the structure are not only effective

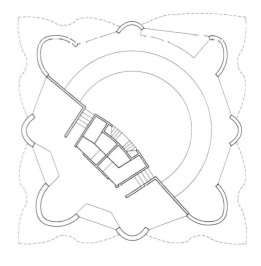

facing page (main picture): Interior of roof of the Naiju Community Center.
facing page (inset): Computer graphic, designing the roof.
above: Plan of the Center.

structurally but make useful openings and alcoves and niches for children to play hide-and-seek and shelter from the rain.

After the success at Naiju, a bamboo-and-concrete structure was used again for the Uchino Community Center. This created a welcoming, soft embracing space for children and elderly people. This multi-purpose facility is intended to establish a bridge between the two diverse age groups, and promote communication and educational exchange. Rather than a grid, the plan is free with a continuous line of perimeter supporting columns. Here, the flowing edge of the roof gives stiffness just like tie bars in ancient vault buildings. The roof form is automatically generated by the plan – the wider the room inside, the higher the roof. The soft edge, like the brim of a hat, sweeps up to deflect rain and dips down to shed water.

This kind of Phenomenological Architecture is extremely flexible. Like the kimono, it can comfortably cover any body shape, or like the furoshiki, it can wrap up any shape via folds, gathers and plaits. It is without doubt rational. On the other hand, the square or rectangle can easily be deformed by changing angles from 90 degrees to any other differential degrees (except for a rigid triangle which never deforms itself). This is similar to the difference between Western principles (hard, clear, crystal) compared with Eastern thoughts (flexible, uncertain, ambiguous and amorphous, like liquid). Chaotic dynamism in the East, rather than static geometry, generates internal forces as time passes. The essence of judo is how to utilize the overwhelming power of the competitor or external force as a counter power to beat or react in turn. It is corresponding external force and internal force.

These Oriental thoughts are reflected in my Phenomenological Architecture. Responding to natural phenomena, it is a deforming process, always temporary, constantly changing, never static, with tremendous diversity. Nothing is permanent or eternal in our Oriental thoughts. One of my intentions is to absorb the shock of change and stress which deforms architecture, and create a "Soft Environment" or an "Architecture in Motion". All architecture is not the same as it was yesterday. It is part of a process of aging, hopefully restored, and exceptionally preserved, as part of natural phenomena. So am I.

Shoei Yoh, Japan

facing page: Uchino Community Center for adults and children. Using computer graphics (inset above), the square gridded bamboo lattice for the roof was deformed into a three-dimensional curved surface, used as a mould in the concrete casting process, and finally left as the interior finish (inset below).

below: Plan of the Center.

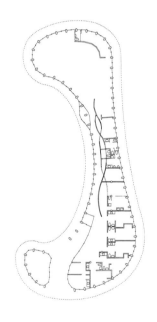

building for life

Imre Makovecz

above: Sketch for the Greek Catholic church, Csenger, Hungary.

facing page: Detail from the centre of the spire at the Catholic church, Szàzhalombàtta, Hungary.

Since earthly man killed off his heavenly predecessors and the earth became the property of Cain's successors; since the angels who brought demonic powers for the first time into the sphere of earthly knowledge entered the abodes of the human daughters – from whose love the giants or Titans sprang; since that time the Sons of Light (as opposed to the Sons of Darkness) have been searching for a way back to nature, back to the world of the Father.

At the end of the 20th and the beginning of the 21st century we too are experiencing this duality. Since the time of William Morris we have seen a resurgence in the organic notion that the purpose of architecture is to connect Heaven and Earth. We must re-evaluate the model of folk art, its bases and ancient wisdom. We must build its millennia-old ideas into our future so that we don't end up going down the wrong path. This is the only way to find our route back to the Golden Age, the only way to liberate ourselves and find a new way back to the Father.

Organic architecture strives to connect the parts of a building which are nearest to the earth – the foundations and walls in particular – closely to the earth. It also strives to construct them from materials which have been extracted from the earth itself. The upper structures should be light, as if heaven were descending upon the earth. Organic architecture combines wilful and abstract forces; it combines flexion and torsion, bringing structure down to pure compression, so that heaven and earth can sit harmoniously with one another.

Our roofs are constructed from wood. We do not believe that wood should be spent in making paper but should be used for doors, windows, floors and roofs. We spend a long time at the construction site, we yield to the earth and

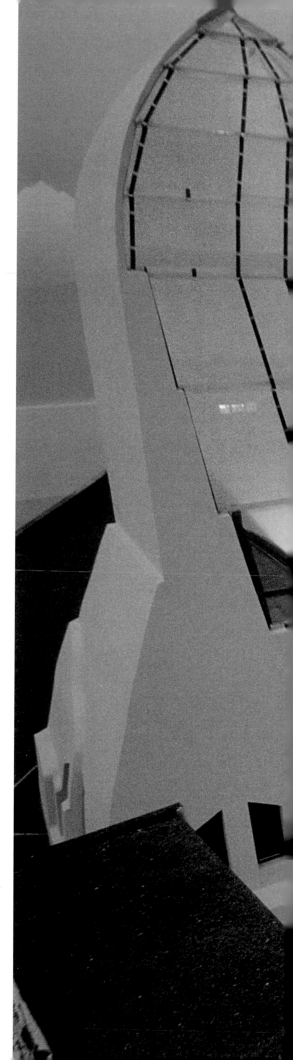

the surroundings, and we also make use of its resources. We are interested in the earth's currents and its waterways.

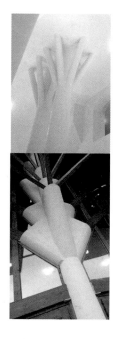

We do not believe in nothingness, blank sheets or pure art. We are not keen on internationalism and globalization. Personal rights are alien to us, as we understand the original meaning of "persona", the Greek "mask". We reject virtual reality, instead struggling on a daily basis to promote experiences based on living archetypes. We did not come onto this earth to inhabit and consume, we came instead to live. Because life is the light of humanity.

Imre Makovecz, Hungary

At the theatre at Makò, the auditorium is flanked by glass towers, pillars soar tree-like to support the wooden roof.

left: Building the wooden framework for

the roof of the Università Cattolica

Auditorium Maximum, Piliscsaba, 1997.

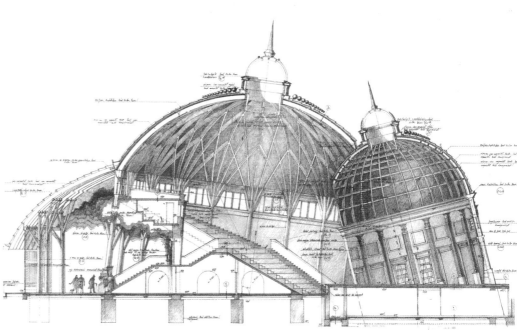

above: Drawing for the Università Cattolica Auditorium Maximum, Piliscsaba, 1997.

John Watson

biostructures

1954, Scottsdale, Arizona, Taliesin West: Frank Lloyd Wright handed me a fly swatter and the essential interview for acceptance as an apprentice at Taliesin began. We decimated the desert flies as the two of us discussed the challenges facing me. Mr Wright said that he would do whatever he could to overcome the

damage that had no doubt been inflicted upon me by my university education. Taliesin was a world of apprenticeship and the only form of architectural education that he believed worthwhile. Although I had read many of Mr Wright's writings it was not until I experienced the daily life and work at Taliesin that I began to grasp the essence of his philosophy. The functional concept of a particular design would come from within. The resultant form and shape would be dictated by the inventive use of materials and new technologies. Self-expression would be stimulated, rather than suppressed, by a client's personality and a particular site.

I certainly found this to be true when I began designing a home for my own budding family in 1968. The design for the residence was inspired by a 270-degree view, and by my own idealistic concept of creating a nest for my as-yet-undeveloped family. The structural system of steel and gunite used for its construction was developed by me in 1959 when I was commissioned to design and construct a small residential dome 36 ft (12 m) diameter.

I had been fascinated by thin shell structures while on a trip to Mexico in the early 50s. Felix Candela* had designed many exciting concrete and steel buildings in that country. Their graceful sculptural shapes had been achieved by the use of elaborate frame scaffoldings and intricate wooden forms. I realized that we could

The Nautilus residence, a gunite dome with bathroom pod, built in Austin, Texas, 1981.

*Felix Candela, *The Shell Builder*, Reinhold Publishing Corporation, New York, 1963

not afford to build complex hyperbolic forms in the United States, so instead of pouring concrete onto wooden forms I used 1 in (25 mm) untested black pipe rolled to prescribed radii to create shapes that became steel armatures for spraying gunite. This new practical use of gunite created a fireproof and tornado resistant structure with a plasticity that could be sculpted into organic forms.

The Nautilus residence at Lake Travis, and the Grotto Dome on Spiller Lane in Austin, are very different examples of this plasticity. The residence at Lake Travis was planted on an unbuildable site that plunged from a shallow shelf to the lake 100 ft (30 m) below. The only possible support for the structure, a reinforced concrete cylinder, contains the circular stairs connecting the living area above to the bedrooms below. The center of this cylinder became the apex of the nautilus producing the expanding radius spiral generation plan. The gunite roof cantilevered across the stair cylinder 14 ft (3.5 m) to shelter the entrance on the street elevation while forming an airplane wing effect over the opposing glazed circular living areas.

The Grotto Dome on Spiller Lane in Austin was designed to complement and reflect a thousand-year-old rock formation in its glass façade. A recirculating waterfall cascades into a pool below the entrance deck, creating an intimate exterior space equal to the interior of the structure itself. A 50 ft (16 m) arched visor of gunite cantilevers over the glass wall and protects the sitting area from sun and rain. Recently a visitor actually commented on how successfully I had created the grotto itself! That was indeed the ultimate compliment to the success of organic architecture.

A current work is inspired by the small mesa site surrounded by cavernous voids and boulders descending to the river. The structure of the residence, though not visible from below, becomes part of the mesa above as it gradually comes into view. This was commissioned because the client had experienced the natural space and the sensitivity of siting of an earlier project. It confirms my belief that organic architecture is ageless, and that it will inspire new ideas and the resultant growth from fertile minds in the 21st century.

John Watson, USA

facing page: Entrance to the Grotto Dome, Austin, Texas, 1980.
above: Spiralling stairs lead from the main living area to the bedrooms in the Grotto Dome.

reclaiming nature

Nature has remained constant during 10,000 years of climatic peace. She has cradled man and allowed him to develop and radically change the world around him. We have learnt to dominate the environment through science and gone down a path of great uncertainty. Humans and our sciences should be desirable rather than detrimental, we have reached a stage where we can and must use our knowledge to reverse some of the damage we have inflicted on nature, and offer a new vision for land development.

Our projects such as the Forest House are as yet theoretical rather than practical, allowing us to race ahead of the current way of practice in order to develop methods to work with environments not only to create architecture but to redefine the science of building. We hope to end up with architecture as close to art as we can make it, understanding how human activity can serve to create infrastructures for more human activity, and addressing, if not reversing, some of the actions which have made the whole prospect of human survival uncertain.

There is no uglier feature on this planet's surface than mass deforestation. We believe that more people resident amongst trees will create more forests. Once we reclaim the forest as an option for everyday life for everyday people, it will once again possess a value well beyond that of planks and paper. The Forest House would be built of timber, stand tall enough to apply for the planet's tallest timber structure record, and provide comfortable accommodation for its occupants while achieving both energy and waste self-sufficiency. Its great height pushes the inhabited sections and those who live in the building into the sun for heat, power and psychological refreshment, plus added benefits of exposure to over-canopy winds to drive an electricity generator and vertical access to structure-mounted greenhouses for food production. In-line reed bed pans would treat liquid wastes, while solids would be collected within a composting toilet providing nutrients for the greenhouses. Additional heat would be available through clean burn coppiced willow in a ceramic stove. As the building is raised on legs this would free the ground for the planting of crops and fruit trees, as well as creating a clearway for the passage of wildlife.

The Forest House would serve as an exemplar structure for a new forest culture where we would be able to use our science to attempt to redress the human position in nature. We could begin to create as part of nature rather than purely as agents for the benefit of the human species.

Steven Johnson, England

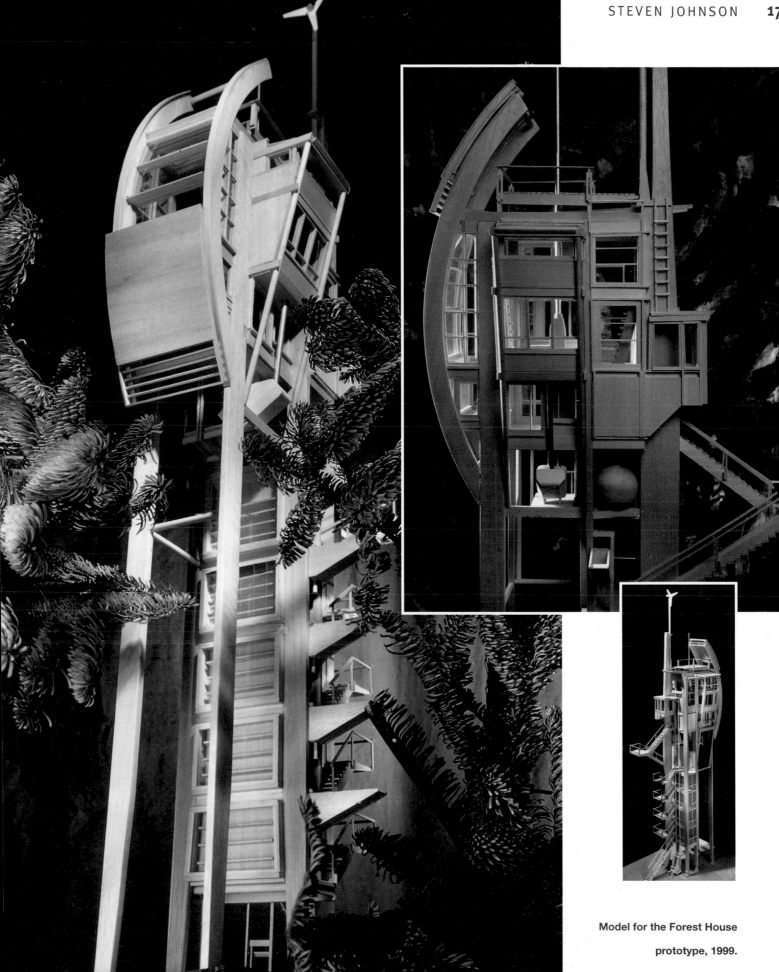

Model for the Forest House

prototype, 1999.

interactive design

Koval

This Pacific coast residence, "The Shark", was designed from the point of view of a child exploring its surroundings. The environment is something to be played with as well as in. Interactive rather than passive, it also plays with you, eliciting reaction from you as you move through it, while also sculpting your movement. If all around you is quiet, and you are clear, you can perceive what each shape feels and how it reacts, when positioned next to another shape, and what kind of feeling that gives the synapse between them. As in the imagination of a child, everything can be, and is, alive.

Cells are individually simple and specialized, put them together and they form a complex, multifunctional whole, an organism. Designing a building in this way is not so much a process of *emulating* nature but of *being* nature. The process itself tends to be tangential, which in a universe where space is curved, means that going off on a tangent will eventually curve you back – perhaps not returning to the same point you started from, but certainly to one which is just as interesting.

This is a kind of zero gravity of the mind. Spaces are not defined so much as they are formed. Lines and places don't really end or begin, they just become more apparent or less apparent, or change, or change direction. As the work evolves within its parameters, it becomes tangible – like air solidifying and becoming visible. Gaps between unconnected elements fill in, as though the connective forms were always there, but not seen. What emerges is formed from something and nothing – both of which are the same thing, in different states. Chaos is a dynamic in this process, and therefore in objective reality, a good thing. Chaos is integral to the universe and to "access" it is to access *ways of flow*, out of which order is sculpted, by inputting energy through skills.

Humans today programme themselves to be desensitized, rarely able to experience full spectrum life radiance, and become confused and antagonistic when exposed to natural aesthetic. It is a humancentric conceit that nature is an adversary to be "controlled" or that it exists for *our* sole benefit. But children that have not been conditioned have an inborn ability to interact with their surroundings without preconception. This enables them to discover the purposes of aesthetic forms at which mere adults would stare blankly, wondering "but what's it for?" "It" is for life. The expression and transmission of aesthetic meaning and depth *is functional*, not a fashionable decoration, or a distraction from "bottom line priorities". When a work is completed successfully, it will appear as though it was incarnated intact, as if it were always meant to be that way.

Koval, Canada

ruled by lines

Keith Struthers

Focusing on external aspects of buildings – whether the walls are straight or curved, for example – completely overlooks something fundamental, namely, how the flatness or curvedness of forms affects our inner condition as human beings. When investigating the effect external phenomena have on our inner self, it helps to focus not only on the end product, but also on the process of creation. Comprehending the creative process itself is in general the unobserved element in our ordinary conceptual life; when creating something our attention is normally not directed towards our own activity, but towards the thing that is being created.

The building is the outward expression of the creative process, and whatever is brought to this process of creation will be experienced by the building's occupants as something that either nourishes or impoverishes them. Whatever inspires and motivates the owners or developers, architects and builders, consciously or unconsciously, during the design and construction process will also, embodied in the very fabric and forms of the building, exert a continuing influence on its inhabitants. In this sense the building is the medium. The end product of the architectural creative process is not the visible structure, but the normally invisible and ongoing evolution of our inner development. Through the catalysing influence of the architectural forms, experiences in the innermost depths of our being are brought to life. This is the real work of art.

In general, mainstream architecture is primarily concerned with physical structures and building styles, whether classical, modern, or organic, expressed in the context of planning arrangements of rooms and spaces. In contrast, a building designed with the explicit intention of developing human faculties only reveals its final form through the inner experiences of human beings. This inner development is neither immediately apparent to external observation, nor subject to the laws of physical matter, hence its elusiveness. Perceiving this non-physical process requires the disciplined development of faculties of cognition over and above those normally thought of as required for designing and constructing buildings.

Consider the difference between the ways in which a violin maker and an architect work. The violin maker cuts the different elements from templates then bends and carves these into the final form of the instrument. The usual method of the architect is to produce line diagrams on flat paper. Models are made by tracing these rectangular diagrams onto cardboard, lifting them into the vertical position, then joining them. By contrast, during the process of making a violin the subtle modulations of the doubly curved surfaces of the bodywork are made visible using bright lights, set up on the sides of the studio at worktop level, to cast shadows and highlight the undulating surfaces. The sculptural form of the surface becomes visible through the interplay of light and shadow. Perception of this relief requires bifocal

**Details of curved rails and a twist in a pillar, in
the Community Development Resource Centre,
Woodstock, Cape Town, South Africa, 1997.**

vision. When looking at the world through a single
eye, we see a flat picture. By combining the two flat
images, each seen from a slightly different angle by
each of our eyes, our sense of spatial depth is created. This also helps us develop the sense that we
occupy a unique position in the world relative to
everyone else and everything surrounding us. Con-
versely a flat surface cannot cast a shadow onto
itself and in this sense does not stimulate bifocal
vision. In so far as each of our eyes is connected to
each half of our brain, we can say single eye vision is
one-sided because it connects to either predominantly left or right brain activity. Producing line diagrams on flat paper requires the use of only a single
colour-blind eye. The plan, section and elevation
"views" are actually thought-diagrams lacking gen-
uine visual content in relation to the buildings they
represent. With the building being made in the
image of these conceptual diagrams, what was sup-
posed to be the means to the end, the flat diagram,
has become the expression of the end itself.

By focusing on how we create, the possibility exists
of becoming aware of both the source of this
process within ourselves, and its potential effect on
others. A design and construction process which
supports the full and healthy expression of our creative capacity is an essential ally to our ongoing spiritual evolution, both personally and socially.

Keith Struthers, South Africa

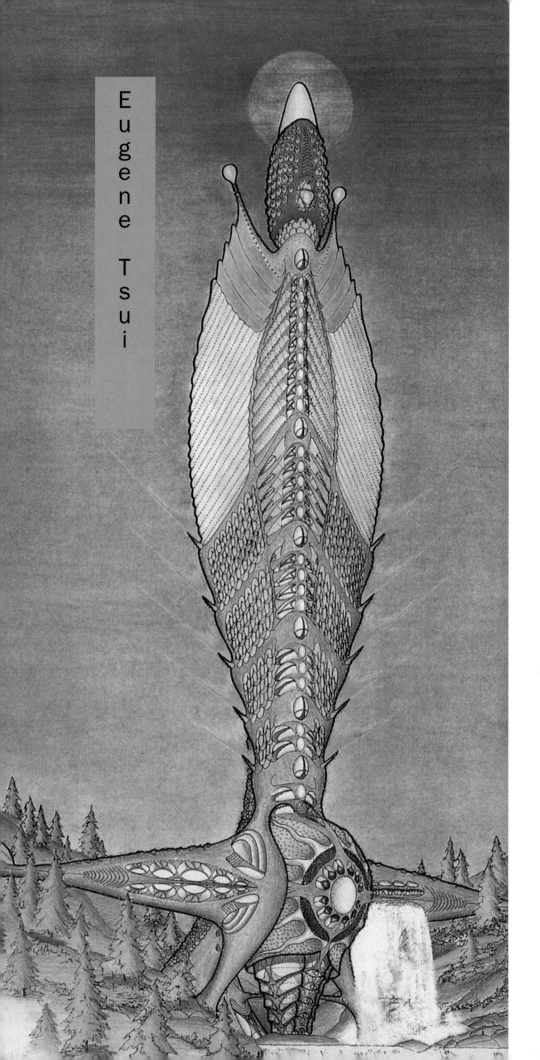

Eugene Tsui

design from nature

Architecture is the timeless and enduring embodiment of a legacy of human dignity. It is the significant physical expression of the deepest and highest aspirations of human life. Yet, through the ages it has commonly neglected the benevolent unity of nature in favor of an exploitative and profiteering mentality. The destruction of our planet illustrates a malady whose only cure lies within the understanding of one simple and universal but often overlooked truth: that we can only live sanely and fully in the presence of nature's bounty and intelligence.

The fish motif recurs in Tsui's architecture, both built and on paper (left). The "Ojo del Sol" (Eye of the Sun) house, Berkeley, California (right and overleaf top), designed for the architect's parents, has fin-like structures, which dissipate rain. Its continuous curvilinear form means the exterior surfaces allow water to drain away so the house needs no eaves, soffits, shingles, or other traditional features. The oval plan makes the house resistant to earthquake shock waves, and the styrofoam/cement block construction is termite proof. The rippling roof attracts maximum sun to heat the interior, and the house repels fire because of its rough texture and round shape.

To create an architecture of meaning and beauty we need to return to the source – nature. We should make use of the materials and innovation provided by the natural world and put them to good use according to their true nature, not merely to imitate the appearances of the past.

The measure by which we advance the knowledge and insight of humanity is inextricably bound to our direct and profound inquiry into the workings of nature. Every "discovery," every incremental improvement of technology, is governed by an insight, a vision, a possibility of some natural phenomenon about to reveal its secrets. Nature is the only continuous and persistent physical presence of god or universal intelligence that we shall ever come to know. Strangely enough, what we do to nature we do to ourselves for we are part of its fabric.

We must remember what we have forgotten: that nature, in its abundant beauty, intelligence and mystery, is a necessary source of life; it is the living force which lies, and has always lain, at the root-core of all human ideas, ingenuity and health. What is of vital importance now is the sensible and imaginative application of the working principles of nature as a way of life. Architecture is instrumental in this. By applying underlying natural principles as a basis for design in our human-made living and working environments we can experience for ourselves the power and beauty of nature's comprehensive design wisdom.

If we observe the human-made landscape which surrounds us we may become aware of the dull, colorless, rigid and impersonal environments we have created for ourselves. Our architecture is too often a benumbing example of questionless convenience and widespread repetition of images steeped in commonplace tradition. Architecture is too often concerned with custom and acceptance, without regard for nature and human dignity. But if we look to the natural world and use nature as the basis for design we can create a new, evolutionary architecture.

Eugene Tsui, USA

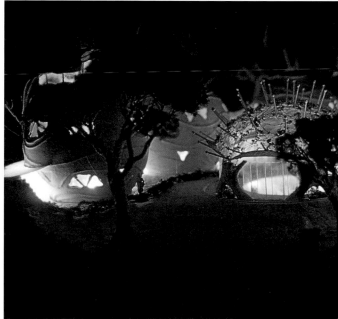

above and right: The Watsu Center is located among the boulders of a northern Californian site. The structures are fireproof, and earthquake-proof, and can be immersed in water. They are passively heated and cooled.

left: The Tsui (Ojo del Sol) house has no stairway but multiple levels inside the eliptical building are reached by a series of ramps which culminate in a central circular ramp at the midpoint of the house.

above: Built in a high risk earthquake zone the Williams extension is a truncated conical structure inspired by the way a barnacle clings to a rock. The small top and large bottom make for a naturally stable geometry and create a self-propelled ventilation system, with no machinery or utility bills.

building Eden

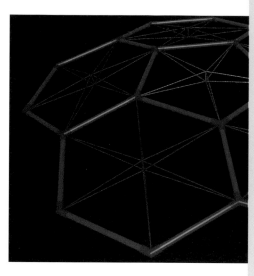

For me, the Eden project starts in London at Paddington Station – an industrial structure built with great innovative spirit in 1854 by Brunel, who in turn was influenced by the famous greenhouse designer, Sir Joseph Paxton. Paddington will, of course, be the start of many people's journey to Eden. From this wonderful structure, recently restored by Nicholas Grimshaw and Partners, begins one of the finest train journeys in Europe which passes through some of England's most spectacular countryside. Between Exeter and St Austell in particular the route encompasses some marvellous spatial and architectural experiences. Travelling along the coast in a southwesterly gale can mean that the sea actually throws itself over the train. Later the train travels through a seaside town, inches from the seafront hotels and holidaymakers. Later still it passes over the River Tamar on Brunel's famous Saltash Bridge – another pioneering structure of great significance. Then onwards, clinging to hillsides where valleys open precipitously away from you, giving a spatial experience which is hard to repeat. After this come woods of wild flowering rhododendrons which seem to be unexplored and uncultivated.

At this point one might ask why this immense botanical centre has been located in Cornwall in a lost valley which was previously a quarry for a particular kind of clay precious to the paper-making and pottery industries. This question can be answered in several ways.

The first is climatic – Cornwall is the warmest part of the British Isles, so that basing this botanical centre in a protected valley in this region gives considerable energy savings. Another, more intriguing, answer is historical. The ports of Cornwall were the first landfalls encountered by many eighteenth- and nineteenth-century sea captains, many of whom collected plant specimens on their

Eden's biomes are a linked series of domes up to 60 m (200 ft) tall constructed of hexagonal cells spanning 9 m (30 ft) across. These climate-controlled transparent capsules hold plants from two climatological regions; the aim of the project is to explore the relationships between plants and humans through science and education.

travels. Some of these plant samples were "dropped off" in Cornwall and found their way to the gardens of the great country houses of the time, such as the gardens of Heligan, since revived and restored, which currently receive 300,000 visitors a year. This leads to the third major reason for the location of the Eden project in Cornwall. A large number of people go to Cornwall for their holidays, so there is a substantial "captive audience" who would welcome an alternative attraction to the traditional day on the beach.

The combination of these locational factors, together with the British history of building greenhouses and wide span structures such as railway stations, makes it clear that Eden is bringing together two traditional British threads – an interest in plants and an interest in structures.

The Eden roof, developed with the structural engineers Anthony Hunt Associates, is a geodesic structure with hexagonal air-inflated transparent foil "pillows" sitting within the galvanized steel frame. I hope that this sophisticated structure will make a fascinating contrast to Paxton's early greenhouses such as the Great Stove and even Crystal Palace, which in spite of its very advanced construction techniques was still a simple, single-glazed enclosure. Our project will also represent a great contrast to Decimus Burton's Palm House at Kew, even though this had many innovative features. As a child, I visited the Palm House on many occasions while staying with my aunt who lived in Richmond. I was intrigued by the structure, the steamy climate and the exotic nature of the plants. However, I was also struck by the somewhat rigid "museum-like" quality created by displaying one specimen of each plant, each religiously recorded with its Latin name.

The idea of learning is a cornerstone of the Eden project, but without the "hands-off" formality of the Victorian era. People arrive first at the visitors' centre, which is designed as a preparation for what they will see in the

The lightweight structure is very flexible, easy to mould to uneven terrain, and suitable for all sorts of ground conditions. Also the domes can be largely fabricated off site and transported piecemeal, making the structure suitable for difficult sites and tight deadlines.

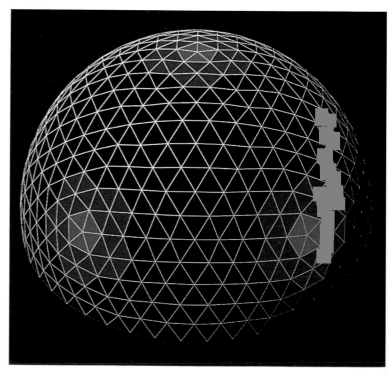

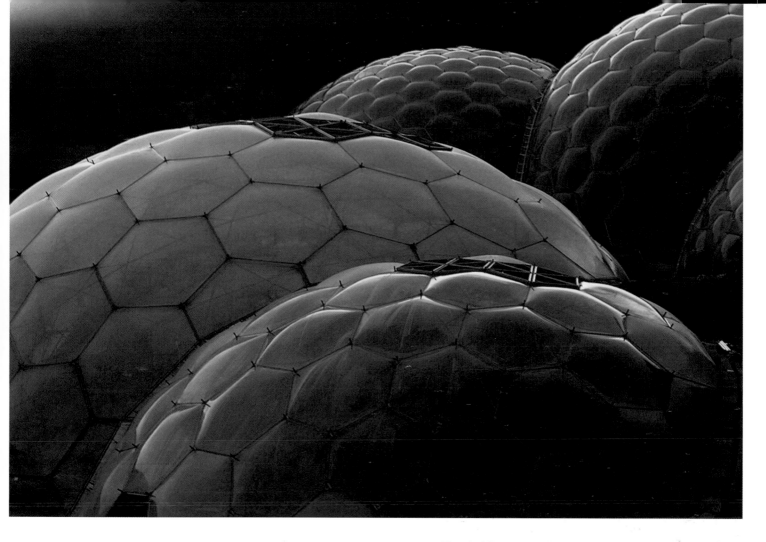

biomes. A winding path leads visitors to an orientation building, which links the climatic zones. The first of these simulates a Mediterranean climate (of particular interest because global warming is apparently causing the areas of the world with this climate to enlarge dramatically). The second biome encloses a tropical rainforest with trees of up to 50 m (160 ft) tall and a waterfall cascading down the face of the existing china clay pit.

The essence of the botanical strategy throughout Eden is to have populations of plants, not just single specimens. This will allow valuable research into issues like mutation and change within plant populations. My own feelings about plants have changed fundamentally since the beginning of the project, and I have become enthralled by the potential range of sensory perception that the architecture of this project could engender.

The cladding system is made of optically clear, air-inflated foil pillows which are 1 per cent the weight of glass. This reduces the overall load on the structure and foundations. As the domes are so light, their stability has to be ensured by sinking foundation supports very deep into the fragmented granite beneath the surface china clay.

It has also made me aware of the important role that plants are now playing in our rapidly-changing world. Plants can no longer be perceived as objects with Latin names in a museum. The survival of the green areas of our planet is now a matter of fundamental importance to everyone. Plants are indeed a matter of life and death for us all. If our project in this lost valley in Cornwall attracts visitors from all over the world, and if they can learn something about the dynamic and changing world of architecture as they learn about the mysteries of the botanical world, then I believe we will have achieved something of which we can all feel proud.

Nicholas Grimshaw, England

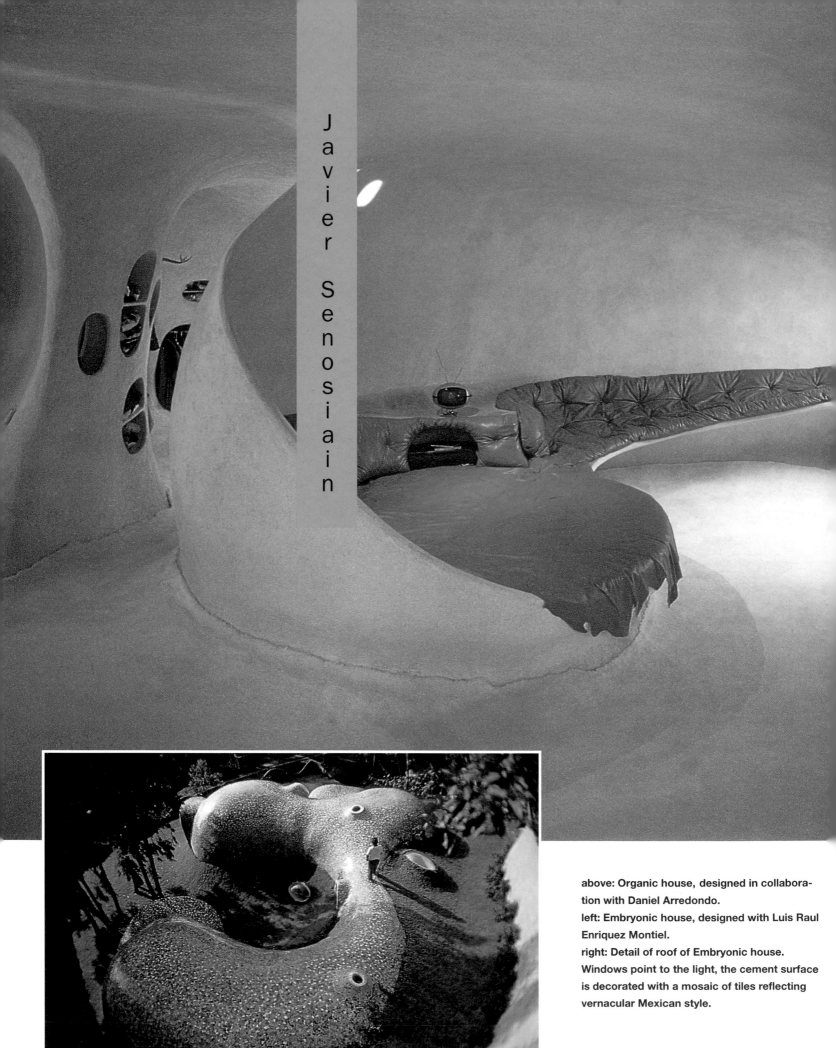

Javier Senosiain

above: Organic house, designed in collaboration with Daniel Arredondo.
left: Embryonic house, designed with Luis Raul
Enriquez Montiel.
right: Detail of roof of Embryonic house.
Windows point to the light, the cement surface
is decorated with a mosaic of tiles reflecting
vernacular Mexican style.

space and harmony

A building should be a space that can adapt to people and is in harmony with the environment. It needs to meet physical and psychological needs, considering humans' origin in nature as well as their organic space throughout history.

The first step for an architect is to put aside any kind of commercial, industrial or conventional interests, as well as any inherited social or academic prejudices regarding architecture. This leaves the door open to choose materials and technologies for their qualities rather than their history. A house should contain continuous ample integral spaces that liberate shapes, strategically placed lighting should follow the natural rhythm of people's movements, and built-in, integrated furniture can facilitate circulation and make the best use of available space. A garden can cover the house, its sloping green "dunes" inviting rest and meditation, and for children to slide down in playful union with the space. Houses become almost invisible, hidden beneath their gardens, with grass, bushes, trees and flowers catching the eye.

I favour the use of a ferrocement structure half buried and covered with a thin layer of soil (so the grass grows more slowly), fluctuating between 15–20 cm (6–8 in) thick. The soil and the grass protect the membrane from the sun, wind, hail and the yearly dry-rainy seasons, so avoiding the stretching that could cause tears and allow humidity to creep in. A double shell of ferrocement needs only one third of the construction material used in a conventional house. Walls need be only 4 cm (1¾ in) thick, and they can be painted straight away whereas bricks or stone have to be plastered first. The shell distributes stresses evenly over the ground so the foundation in itself is the equivalent to the reinforced foundation of a conventional structure. Another advantage is the greater capacity for load transfer, as the monolithic structure is stronger and more efficient than conventional construction.

The thermal characteristics of city surfaces are completely different from those in a purely natural environment; and the penetration, reflection and absorption of light are also quite different. Meadows, trees and bushes help maintain thermal balance in the atmosphere, so the microclimate of a semi-buried

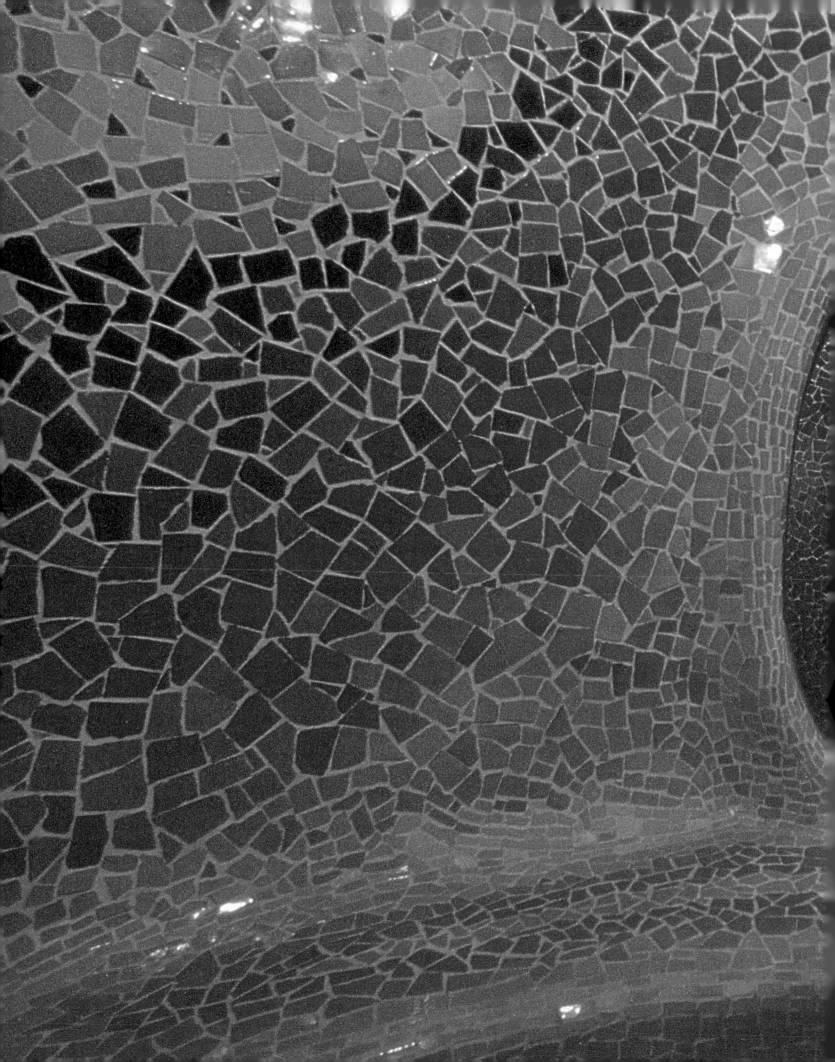

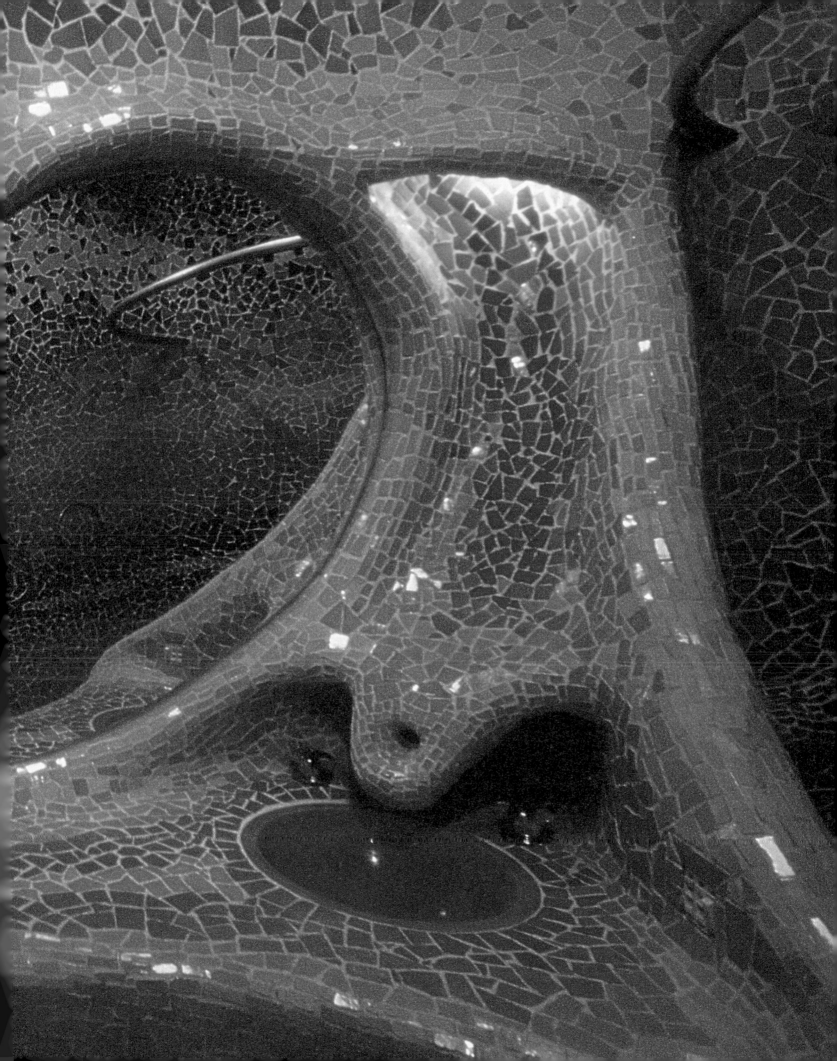

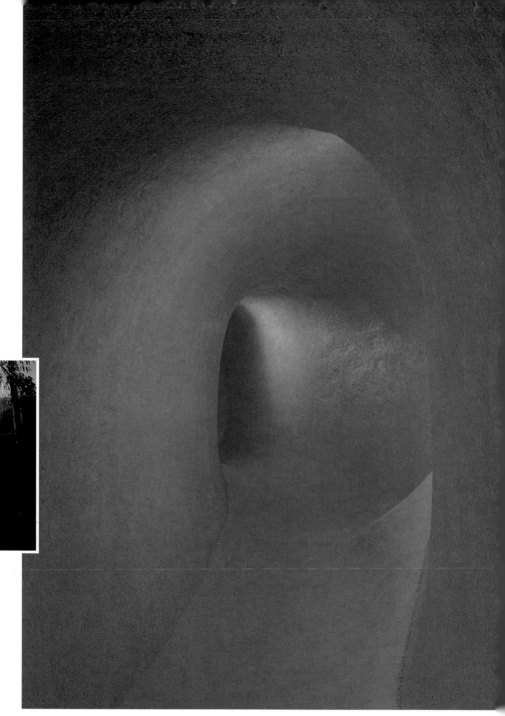

grass-covered building means efficient cooling and heating, and the green barriers of the garden filter direct sunlight and create shadows that protect the home from heat, dust and noise. They also refresh the atmosphere

with evaporation and transpiration of the foliage. The earth and sun work together to maintain a stable temperature inside the house where the earth offers protection and the sun provides light and warmth. Windows should be oriented toward the most attractive views, preferably facing south for sunlight in winter, seeking light like a plant does. This kind of underground home is well-lit and full of sunshine as its windows may point in any direction and the domes allow light and sunshine in from above. Ventilation is easy as the aerodynamic shapes of the dwelling make for free circulation of air. In the same way that the internal temperature of our bodies remains stable even though the outside temperature varies, this happens in buried homes. The soil

moderates the cooling and warming effects above the earth, and the house maintains a constant temperature range of 18–23°C all year long, warm in the winter and cool in the summer. Throughout the year the microclimate conserves an average relative humidity of 40–70 per cent, protecting inhabitants from respiratory illnesses and complications.

In projects such as "The Organic House" we want to attain spaces that adapt to the

previous page: The tiled mosaic bathroom of the Embryonic house.

above, left, and right: The Shark house, designed with Luis Raul Enriquez Montiel, resembles a shark emerging from the landscape; inside spaces flow smoothly into each other, furniture is integrated, light filters from above.

from exterior fires, and the ferrocement structure is practically incombustible. Soil is also a magnificent acoustic insulation.

Access to the house is through the mouth of a snail. A periscope at the entrance allows whoever is in the kitchen to see who rings the bell. The inside of the house is reached by descending through the snail into the tunnel and to the living room, to areas for eating and cooking, and on to the furthest sleeping area.

Furniture was built in all over the house according to analysis of daily needs. In the kitchen there are burners, a sink and built-in shelves for the pantry. In the bedroom are more cubbyholes for putting away clothes, while in the bathroom the taps of the basin, shower, and bath tub are waterfalls. In the living room the carpet stretches over a filling of small polyurethane balls which conform to the shape of whoever is seated there, organically accommodating a person to the floor in the same way an animal sprawls out. In earlier times humans were more rooted to the earth, more in contact and in harmony with her, a relationship that has been lost in our urban environment, our architecture reconciles the best from ancient and modern.

Javier Senosiain, Mexico

human body, like the womb or an animal's lair. Like the troglodytes who carved a niche for themselves out of the earth, or igloo builders, this is not a regression to primitive ways but a premeditated reconciliation. This type of house is not only a private retreat but also a refuge from the elements: a free-shaped buried house proffers little resistance to the wind but it is unaffected by earthquakes. And if a tall heavy tree fell on the house it would not affect the structure as the soil would absorb the shock of the impact. External grass and soil protect the house

Kendrick Bangs Kellogg

working with nature

Walking down the hall of the University of Colorado's department of architecture in 1955 I came upon a picture of Frank Lloyd Wright's Fallingwater. I was a second-year student there and had attended three schools of architecture, but up to that time I had no idea of just how beautiful architecture could be, or that there was a way of thinking about architecture that was complementary with nature and at the same time expressive of our time.

Why hadn't the schools shown me this direction earlier? And why were schools not encouraging young hungry minds to quest for the opportunity of creative thinking? It was a common problem then, and from what I have heard from many students, it remains so today.

The idea of organic architecture was not originated by Frank Lloyd Wright. As early as the 18th century architects were beginning to protest against conformity and non-functionality in architecture and planning. He merely carried it to a new level, emphasizing how "form and function are one". The overused cliché that "form follows function" is a trap. Beyond the discipline of architecture the "ordinary" is the problem we all face in our lives, where ordinary forms perform expected functions. A box can serve as a house and fulfil its expected functions. That's the trap. But in architecture, as in life, every site creates opportunities for fighting what is "ordinary". There need be no place for "ordinary". Organic architecture encompasses the idea that beauty and practicality always go hand-in-hand.

High Desert home, Palm Springs, California. On the south slope of a large rock outcrop, gently curved concrete wings rest on cantilevered platforms, resembling a prehistoric bird rising out of the landscape. The earthquake-proof home is designed for energy gains from the thermal mass. A subterranean garage protects the natural landscape.

above and left: An earth form studio at the Institute of Organic Architecture, Mount Paloma. This ongoing project is being constructed with students learning how to design and build original architecture symbiotic with Nature.

right: Concrete arches spring from the rock to form the Hoshino Wedding Chapel, Japan. Marble floors and cherry wood pews finish the interior.

To realise truly creative architecture you need clients with the vision and imagination to make the most of any site. Great clients are those who allow an architect the latitude to give them what they didn't know they wanted until they have it! They are willing to risk being unique. The Hoshino Wedding Chapel in Japan is a good example, built for a client with a great sense of quality and beauty, and a desire to circumvent the restrictions of society. This much used rock and concrete chapel is a successful and popular example of architecture built for future generations.

One of my favorite remodeling projects took a badly-proportioned box of a house on a beautiful winding road in Del Mar overlooking the Pacific Ocean, and transformed it into a living home. We realigned the contours of the house to be more consistent with the approach from the curving road and to blend with the cliff-like terrace; the house's sinuous curves now complement the site. The emotional impact is such that the owners experience a "catch in the throat" each time they drive around the corner to rediscover the house.

Organic architecture is living architecture. It should emphasize the potential and environmental fulfilment of individual experience and expression as an intrinsic necessity of our survival. Our sense of individual expression is our inalienable right, but we must equip ourselves with the right tools to be able to express ourselves. Work experience, apprenticeships and construction internships are important so that

The roof of the Yen House at La Jolla, California, is designed with integral solar panels (left). Inside (above) a web of roof beams join pillars which cantilever through to the roof and also act as window frames.

we understand how to eke the most from our designs. In my own experience overseeing construction projects, I've heard workers proclaim that they've been doing their job for 30 years and know what they're doing. But I can tell them "I've been doing this for 40 years and I still don't know what I'm doing, but if you can't do it, I will." I favor hands-on training and work-related programs for all students, stressing first-hand experience of architecture as symbiotic with nature, my life's passion. The ongoing construction program at the Institute of Organic Architecture represents the importance of the participatory learning process of designing and building with nature.

Above all, organic architecture should constantly remind us not to take Mother Nature for granted – work with her and allow her to guide your life. Inhibit her, and humanity will be the loser.

Kendrick Bangs Kellogg, USA

In the centre of the historic 12th-century city of Zutphen, the Netherlands, the new City Hall sits comfortably within the past. The design and materials were heavily influenced by the wishes of the townspeople for a "transparent, pleasant, efficient, active and responsible" building. The history and archaeology of the town and the dynamic between old and new were crucial design factors, combined with the architect's vision of movement in space as the key to architecture.

T
h
o
m
a
s

R
a
u

value in architecture

Set up in 1992, from the start the social value of every project has been integral to Thomas Rau & Partners' approach. This goal is also reflected in our internal office organisation where we have an open, horizontal structure with everyone working with their specific expertise towards the communal goal. The non-material dimension is not forgotten, the desire to create buildings in which and through which people feel good.

Work as development

Every assignment is seen as an opportunity to develop further as people and architects. So we start every project by asking ourselves what scope it offers for professional and personal development. We are continually looking for new challenges and carrying out research which means that you could almost say that our product is completely renewed every five years. Within a project's framework, we always try to create space for personal development, as pure intellectualism can be the kiss of death for spirituality.

This constant search for new ways of working is particularly focussed on the way in which architecture makes use of natural resources.

Two themes are constant: building sustainability and energy-saving construction. These themes should be seen as completely integral to all architecture. It is totally unacceptable for an architect to boast about sustainability; every client should be able to assume that an architect has the latest developments in that area ready and integrated in his project. After all, an architect does not brag about the fact that he can build weatherproof structures!

Designing for people and planet

Our interest in sustainability leads us to explore the possibilities for achieving the so-called "autonomous building" – or preferably, a building that produces more energy than it uses. We are convinced that this need not mean additional costs, but is more a question of moving budgets around. It does mean that our advisers have to be able to collaborate in the integral thinking process central to all our work.

We are also trying to create buildings that provide energy in a non-material sense. The underlying idea is clear: a building in which people feel good will last longer and is therefore more sustainable. This quality of durability is too often ignored, with sustainability questions usually revolving around quantifiable aspects of a building such as techniques or materials.

The underlying concept of our buildings is designing for people to feel good, and we care how materials effect people through their form and colour as well as their physical properties – different forms affect the energetic appearance of a material. In our buildings every material, form and colour is part of the total concept. We are aware of our great responsibility to our clients in providing buildings that provide social and spiritual as well as physical quality, and it is a misconception that this has to mean increased expense, we make very valuable buildings in the sense that they have received a lot of attention, but that doesn't have to mean high prices. Delivering maximum quality within an agreed budget is an art which we are constantly exploring.

Architecture as discourse

Dialogue with the client is very important in every matter. Discussions begin with the collaborative development of a concept for the building. This preliminary stage, the ideas phase, is the most important. The clients' input is vital, without it we could not get a properly focussed picture of the building's requirements. Great attention is paid to the presentation stage, and during our discussions we strive for the "authority" of the concept, agreed principles and intentions against which every new suggestion is carefully checked. This agreed overall concept is crucial, as ultimately it is neither the stubbornness of the architect, nor the personal preferences of the customer, but adherence to the concept that provides the final decision.

Thomas Rau and Partners, the Netherlands

The design of the Triodos bank in Zeist, the Netherlands, was influenced by the aim to construct a building that was the most sustainable low-energy building possible, as well as one that is inspiring to work in and visit. Contrasting shapes and materials on the façades and the interiors symbolize the "hard" business side of banking and the "soft" side, involving consideration for people and the environment.

Arthur Dyson

defining space

As an architect, I have found the best way to deliver an effective design is to listen. Clients who seek my services have already made numerous decisions that determine what will best serve their needs. Many of these conscious choices may be long forgotten into preferred habits of living and working, or perhaps distilled into the sentiments of anniversaries. By hearing of personal histories and preferences, such as music and art, a deeper sense of boundaries and engagements with life becomes clear. Clients bring their architecture with them. My goal is to discern this self-knowledge and render a structure that, something like a trellis, sustains their lives and supports future growth.

One of the most telling elements of an architectural design is the location where the structure will be built. The inclinations and limitations of the client have intersected at a geographical location. Much about the architecture of a potential building has already been determined by topography and climatic conditions. My task is to match the unavoidable with the desirable in a balance that is at the same time static and dynamic.

The workings of built architecture can take place only within the context of the natural environment. Human existence is inescapably bound up into the processes of this larger living system. Designs that accommodate the necessities and desires of people must relate comprehensively to a vast arena of ongoing forceful interplay: indeed. architecture arises fundamentally as a response to the surrounding world. Whether a building is more or less successful depends on the extent to which this awareness is expressed.

Architecture is the act of defining place. Sites are at the same time both physical and psychological. The relationships between the inner and the outer worlds of experience are constantly moving moments of human response. Physically these functions intertwine in balances of hot and cold, light and dark, solid and void. At the same

Jaksha residence, Madera County, California, 1988. The use of large overhangs and trellises allows enjoyment of the sunsets while providing protection from the hot sun.

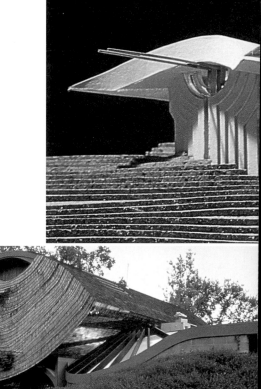

instant, the mind reflects succour or discomfort, satisfaction or unpleasantness, success or failure. Ironically this effervescent effect has to occur through a fixed, unchanging placement of building materials. Architectural forms are the crystallized rendering of potential states of being. For me this is the poetry of architecture. The cycles of the earth provide a recurring sense of happenings, phrases of passage that can invoke patterns of certainty. Seasonal changes bring emotional moods, night and day punctuate perception and reflection. Buildings emerge to solidify these relationships of identity in what Louis Sullivan called "The Great Life". Architecture serves as the medium of what we are to become by showing us who we are. We take our place by virtue of the greater environment out of which we have already arisen.

Yet, whatever our context within a larger matrix, we are also individuals. Something about human nature requires unique expression for complete fulfilment. Good architecture cannot escape meeting this requirement. Each architectural form is a separate and discrete creation; this presents a fresh chance for creative response each and every time. Even when underlying, criteria are parallel, there are always going to be variations to evoke between one design and another.

In the biological world there are many similar forms, yet there is also distinction. Colour and specialised development of feathers in birds is a good example, another is easily seen in the rich diversity of flowers. As in nature, selecting the right point of emphasis for enrichment in an architectural design is neither capricious or wasteful. The result should be inspiring, while in perfect harmony with the entire composition.

Functional logic in design also demands economic responsibility. For many clients the opportunity to build is a major financial venture. A successful design will provide a uniform quality of presence that maximises available resources. Sometimes works must be completed over a period of years, rather than all at once, in order to achieve the best result. This too is a reflection of the growing natural world. An effective architectural design will inevitably come to good account for the money, however long the time needed.

The philosophy that drives my work is rooted in principles that take the metaphor of the organic world. This architectural approach was first articulated in America by Louis Sullivan. As a

above: Lencioni residence, Sanger, California, 1985. A beam raised onto the foundation anchors the house in a grassy carpet, setting the whole composition comfortably on the ground. The flowing shape of these curves establishes the sinuous form of the exterior surface finished in red cedar shingles.

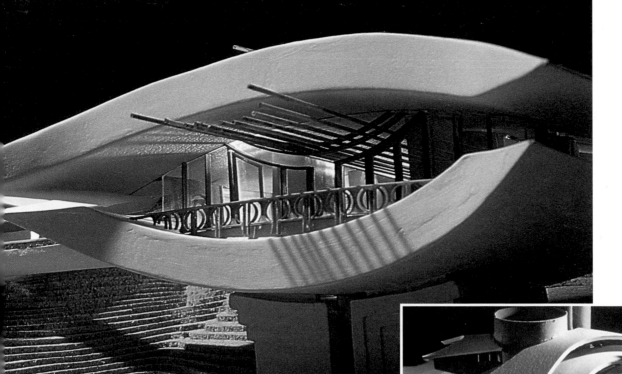

below: Hilton residence, Panama
City Beach, Florida, 1999. The
primary rooms of this residence,
nestling in the dunes on the Gulf
of Mexico, are suspended on
concrete pads at various levels.
Tiered roof wings sweep upward,
forming a series of clerestories.

**above: Newving residence,
Greensboro, North Carolina, 1988.
This two-bedroom home is a wood-
framed structure with cement plaster
finish. The interior is illuminated from
early morning to evening through the
window wall of the south elevation.
The arched ceiling is tempered by a
trellis of copper pipes reaching outward framing prospective vistas.**

young man I apprenticed at various times with later adherents of his organic theses, including Frank Lloyd Wright, Bruce Goff, and William Gray Purcell. All of these masters used their long careers to emphasise the importance of honesty in architectural expression. They saw this as a spiritual, but not dogmatic, quest that was inherent in every single building.

I hope that I have carried on some of their enthusiasm and commitment to human betterment through careful architectural choice.

In the rush of the modern world we are ironically often left feeling isolated, yet at the same time weary of demands. This conflict is fundamentally a spiritual one, something that in the mode of organic design has potential architectural solutions. Each of us has a unique and vital contribution to make to the larger human community. In turn, the body politic can only become healthier and stronger for all that participate. My role as an architect is to help people reach for a preferred future from wherever they can start out.

Arthur Dyson, USA

Philippe Samyn

The ovoid form of the Walloon Branch of Reproduction Forestry Material was chosen initially because of the polygon shape of the site, which is timbered with old oaks. The structure is a framework of composed arcs made of rectangular pieces of bent green wood, each over 6 m (19 ft) long. Large tiles of laminated reflecting glass cover the wooden shell.

material geometry

The projects of Samyn and Partners, architects and engineers, are based on a clear morphological pattern using mainly local materials and technology. Our projects are global and include landscaping and interior fit-out as well as structure. The design approach is based on questioning.

The inquisitive approach often leads us to discover unconventional answers to an identified question. To me, the built environment results from the use of geometry and materials to respond to physiological needs in a given environment – which includes the site, the programme, the socio-economic and historical context. The specific geometrical pattern of the site along with this "environment" are at the roots of every architectural response, which must therefore always be unique and site-specific; no two sites will yield the same broad environmental conditions.

One experiment after another leads to certain convictions that are then codified to support the questioning. This question and discovery process leads our team to focus on differing areas of interest including structural morphology and building physics. We are committed to respecting nature, and concentrate on trying to build inexpensively and using minimum energy at every stage. This commitment always implies the use of local skills, materials and technology and leads to sustainable architecture.

The field of structural morphology is a prime interest in this search for inexpensive and light structures. My recent researches concern harmonic structures, trusses with meshes of variable sizes including the Internally Stayed Truss, the fractals of the regular polygons on double curved surfaces, and internally damped structures.

Next to geometry, the choice of materials influences the concept of structures. Circumstances lead us to use a great variety of materials including fabrics and wood. The first mainly because of its low cost and speed of erection, the second for its ease of use and compatibility with interior design and thus its "liveability".

Since 1987 we have been involved in the design of various fabric structures that led us to develop stiff transparent fabrics. Our first built fabric structure was in 1989–1991 to cover the M&G Research Laboratory in Venafro-Isernia, Italy. Two awnings to cover the FINA petrol stations on the E411 Motorway in Belgium followed it. Another design was created to cover the aerial metro station "Erasmus" in Brussels.

From the smallest shed to the largest of buildings, wood structures are long lasting if properly protected from moisture and rain. All the design effort in wooden structures is centred on connections and the way to deal with the limited transversal strength and stiffness of wood. We favour "parallel" structures, whose global stability does not depend on every single structural component; they allow for simple detailing (due to the dissipation of the forces) and the use of wood whose grade does not need to be severely checked.

In 1987, the competition for the extension of the Banque Bruxelles-Lambert in Brussels led us to study a "double skin" façade for the first time. It was followed by other initially unsuccessful proposals, but in 1993 we finished construction of the Brussimmo building in Brussels' main business district. Its double clear glass skin allows significantly reduced operating costs compared to a classical office building.

The concept of "intermediate spaces" was used for the M&G Research Laboratory in Venafro, and for various subsequent projects, by using the intermediate space between the outer and inner skin to house functions that do not need great temperature control. It allows mechanical cooling to be limited to some of the internal rooms or even to be totally suppressed when the free cooling effect is used. We also followed this principle in the Walloon Branch of Reproduction Forestry Material. This has led us naturally further to develop the concept of "free cooling" which we have used in many recent projects, building on our growing experience of double skins and intermediate spaces. Careful day lighting considerations have also greatly influenced our designs.

So what next? The extraordinary evolution of computer software and hardware increasingly fosters new approaches to design, allowing architects and engineers to study every aspect of buildings and respond ecologically to the requirements.

Philippe Samyn, Belgium

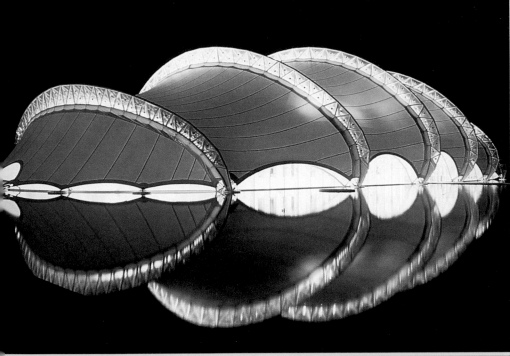

The M&G Research Laboratory at Venafro, Italy, is a light tent-like form placed in the centre of a rectangular reflective pool for security, thermal regulation, and to enhance the form and the landscape with its reflections and coolness.

The PVC coated polyester membrane is supported by a symmetrical arched metal trellis held by six longitudinal suspension cables. The space is lit from within as well as by the perimeter steel-framed and arched window.

Selected biographies

Note: This section contains biographical information where supplied on the architects featured in Part 2 of this book.

Fabrizio CAROLA

Born in Naples in 1931, Carola gained a diploma from the National Higher School of Architecture, Brussels (La Cambre) in 1956. Carola has worked in France, Cameroon, Mali, Mauritius, Guatemala, Burkina Faso, Senegal, Togo, and Latin America, as well as his native Italy. His many built projects, public and private, concentrate on using materials and technologies that are appropriate to the environment and the culture. In 1995 he received the Aga Khan Award for Architecture for his hospital at Kaedi, Mauritania (see page 83). He has also designed interiors and stage sets, including work with Werner Herzog on his 1987 film *Green Cobra*.
http://216.121.173.246

Bart PRINCE

Bart Prince was born in Albuquerque, New Mexico, and lived in several New Mexico towns such as Santa Fe, Espanola, and Albuquerque during his formative years. His first building designs for which he received awards were made at the age of seven and his first houses were built in Albuquerque while he was attending high school. He studied architecture at Arizona State University, Tempe and began working for architect Bruce Goff prior to graduating. After receiving his degree in architecture he continued his work with Goff in Missouri and Texas until returning to Albuquerque in 1973 to start his own practice. Prince has lectured and taught widely in the USA, Canada, England, France, Austria, Australia, Costa Rica, Iraq, and Japan.
www.bartprince.com

Jacques GILLET

Born in 1931 in Liège, Belgium, Jacques Gillet studied at the Liège Upper Institute of Architecture. His research and teaching has focused on organic architecture. He was Professor of Architecture at Liège Upper Institute of Architecture from 1964 until 1997. In 1978 he founded the first European course on Organic Architecture at the Lambert Lombard Institute in Liège, where he is now Emeritus Professor of Architecture. He has been adviser to many organizations including the Friends of Kebyar, and has spent several years working in the USA, France, and Switzerland. He has written and contributed to numerous publications. Awards have included: Great Prize of Liège for Architecture (1956); Great Prize of Rome for Architecture (1963); Picard Prize from the Free Academy of Belgium (1968); recognition by the King of Belgium for "professional and scientific excellence" (1983). Some examples of his work can be see on:
www.kebyar.com

Erik ASMUSSEN

Born in Copenhagen in 1913, Asmussen studied architecture in Copenhagen. In 1939 he moved to Stockholm and worked for various architects there. From 1942 until 1960 he was employed by the firm of Nils Tesch and Lars Giertz. He then started working on his own, with the Kristoffer School and in 1976 moved to Järna, south of Stockholm. His practice was awarded several prizes, including the Prins Eugens Medal, in 1991. His work was exhibited at the Royal Academy of Fine Arts in 1998. In August of the same year Asmussen died. His co-workers continue his work under the name of "Asmussens Arkitektgrupp AB", at the same office in Järna.
www.asmussens.se

Douglas CARDINAL

Douglas Cardinal has been building "indigenous-style" buildings in Canada and elsewhere since the 1960s. He has received many awards, including Great Canadian Award (1992); Canada Council Molson Prize for the Arts (1992 and 1993); National Aboriginal Achievement Award, Canada (1995); the Caledonian Prize Lectureship, Edinburgh, Scotland (1997); the Royal Architectural Institute of Canada Gold Medal (1999). He was nominated as Canada's "Living Treasure" for the 1990 New Zealand Sesquicentennial Year Celebrations.
www.dcardinal.com

Gregory BURGESS

Born in 1946 in New South Wales, Burgess graduated with a BA in Architecture from the University of Melbourne in 1970. He established his practice in 1983, since when he has created a reputation for innovative, economical, and popular building solutions. Gregory Burgess has taught widely throughout Australia, he has contributed to many publications, and his practice has received numerous top awards from the Royal Australian Institute of Architects and other bodies, reflecting in particular their concern with cultural and environmental as well as aesthetic context.
e-mail: gbarch@ozemail.com.au

Sim VAN DER RYN

Through his varied experience as principal of several design firms, Professor of Architecture at the University of California, Berkeley, and California State Architect, Sim Van der Ryn has provided numerous examples of ecological design. As President and Chief Designer at Van der Ryn Architects in Sausalito, California, he is currently designing a new generation of environmentally friendly buildings. The American Institute of Architecture designated his Real Goods Solar Living Center in Hopland, California as one of the nation's top ten projects for Earth Day 1999. His recent design for the West End Golden Gate Park Pavilion Community Center is the pilot project for the city of San Francisco's Green Building Initiative. Van der Ryn is author of several books, including *Sustainable Communities* (1986), *Ecological Design* (with Stuart Cowan, 1996), and *Geometry of Hope* (2000). www.vanderryn.com

Eric FURNEMONT

Born in 1962 in Liège, Belgium, Eric Furnémont graduated in 1985 with distinction from the Liège Upper Institute of Architecture, where he had studied under Jacques Gillet (*qv*). From 1985 to 1989 he worked with several architectural practices in Belgium. During this time he developed his interest in and experience of buildings that respect ecology and the environment. Eric Furnémont is also involved in teaching and international workshops on a variety of architecture-related topics. He has contributed to many architectural publications and his work has been exhibited in Belgium, Sweden, and Switzerland, and most recently at "Bois et Habitat", Namur, 1999/2000. e-mail: eric.furnemont@village.uunet.be

Daniel LIEBERMANN

Born in 1930 in Princeton, New Jersey, Liebermann studied architecture at Johns Hopkins University and later at Harvard under Serge Chermayeff and Stanley White. He went on to study at the University of Colorado. He was Frank Lloyd Wright Fellow at Taliesin East and West (1956–58). In 1958 he founded his own practice with Eva Liebermann, Gero Martin, and Donald Hoppen and in the ensuing years pioneered passive solar, seismic, wind, and eco site responsive architecture in California and abroad. From 1966 to 1975 he travelled widely in Europe and the USA, undertaking a variety of design commissions and academic posts. He has contributed to numerous architectural and design publications in the USA and Europe.

Balkrishna DOSHI

Doshi was born in 1927 in Pune, India. He studied at the J J School of Architecture, Bombay, and established the Vastu-Shilpa Foundation for Studies and Research in Environmental Design in 1955. He has worked in the USA and Europe since 1958 as well as in India, and has held important chairs in American universities. He was the first Director of the School of Architecture, Ahmedabad (1962–72), then Founder Director of School of Planning and Centre for Environmental Planning

and Technology, Ahmedabad from 1972. Doshi has received many honours, including: M.B Achwal Memorial Gold Medal of the Indian Institute of Architects (1988); Great Gold Medal for Architecture, Academy of Architecture, Paris (1988); Vishwa Gurjari Award (1988); Aga Khan Award for Architecture (1995). He is a Fellow of the Royal Institute of British Architects, Fellow of the Indian Institute of Architects, and Honorary Fellow of the American Institute of Architects www.indiabuildnet.com/arch/sangath_15.htm

Tadao ANDO

Born in 1941 in Osaka, Japan, Tadao Ando was self-educated in architecture. In 1969, after travelling in Europe, Africa, and the USA he established his own architectural firm. His works include Church of the Light, Ibaraki, Osaka (1989); Japan Pavilion, Expo '92, Seville (1992); Meditation Space, UNESCO, Paris (1995); Toto Seminar House, Awaji Island, Hyogo (1997). He has been Visiting Professor at Yale, Columbia, and Harvard Universities in the USA, and in 1997 was appointed Professor at Tokyo University. His awards include the Alvar Aalto Medal, Finnish Association of Architects (1985); Gold Medal of Architecture, French Academy of Architecture (1989); Pritker Architecture Prize (1995); Royal Gold Medal, Royal Institute of British Architects (1997).

Drew HUBBELL

Drew Hubbell was one of the first architects in southern California to use strawbales as a building material. He specializes in environmentally sustainable architecture and the use of alternative construction materials, such as adobe and sprayed concrete, as well as straw bales. His designs include private homes, a Quaker meeting house, a building for the San Diego Zoo Wild Animal Park, and an environmental learning centre in Mexico. He was educated at the Danish Institute of study in Copenhagen and at the University of Arizona. His design vocabulary stems from extensive travel in Europe, Asia, and the USA. Drew Hubbell is a member of Citizens Coordinate for Century 3, an organization that works on San Diego's Master Plan; the California Straw Bales Association (CASBA), the Sustainable Community Action Network (SCAN); and the Newschool Arts Foundation Board. He has been in partnership with the artist James Hubbell since 1994.

James T. HUBBELL

James Hubbell is a sculptor, painter, stained glass artist, poet, visionary, and designer. He has designed chapels, sacred gardens, parks, schools, bed and breakfast inns, restaurants, and private homes in the USA, Mexico, and Russia. Examples of his art can be found all over the world. His awards include the American Institute of Architects Orchid Award; an honorary professorship from the Far Eastern State Technical

University in Vladivostok Russia; and the Interfaith Forum on Religion, Art, and Architecture Award for excellence in design. www.sandiegoart.com/JHubbell

Vitor Ruivo FORTE

Born in 1956 in Mozambique. Following a brief stay in Portugal, he moved to Liège, Belgium, where he studied architecture with Jacques Gillet (qv). In 1983, he moved to Portugal and started his career as an architect. His designs have included single and multi-residential facilities, religious buildings, hotels, commercial complexes, and recreational facilities. He is presently fulfilling a lifelong ambition to design his own home.

Renzo PIANO

Renzo Piano was born in Genoa in 1937 into a builder's family. He graduated from the School of Architecture, Milan Polytechnic in 1964. From 1965 to 1970 he worked with Louis I. Kahn in Philadelphia, USA, and Z. S. Makowsky in London, England. From 1971 he collaborated with Richard Rogers and from 1977 with Peter Rice. He currently runs his own building design firm, Renzo Piano Building Workshop. His major projects include Centre Georges Pompidou (with Richard Rogers), Paris (1977); S. Nicola football stadium, Bari (1990); Columbus International Exposition, Genoa (1992); Jean Marie Tjibaou Cultural Center, Nouméa (1998); Potsdammer Platz reconstruction, Berlin (1999); Padre Pio Pilgrimage Church, Foggia, in progress. In 1998 he was awarded the Pritzker Architecture Prize.
www.renzopiano.com

Eisaku USHIDA

Born in Tokyo, Ushida attended the University of Tokyo 1972–76. From 1976 until 1982 he worked at Arata Isozaki & Associates. In 1984 he joined Richard Rogers Partnership and in 1986 he founded his own practice with Kathryn Findlay (qv).

Kathryn FINDLAY

Born in Scotland, Findlay studied at the Architectural Association, London (1973–79). She joined Arata Isozaki & Associates in 1980 and later undertook postgraduate studies at the University of Tokyo. In 1986 she co-founded Ushida Findlay Partnership with Eisaku Ushida.

Mickey (G.K.) MUENNIG

Born in Joplin, Missouri, in 1935. Muennig attended the Georgia Institute of Technology and later moved to the University of Oklahoma to study under Bruce Goff. After serving apprenticeships, he established and ran his own architectural practice in Missouri for five years. His Foulke House built at this time was highly acclaimed. He then moved to an architectural firm in Denver, Colorado, where he worked on a variety of large housing projects. In 1971 he set up a new private practice in Big Sur, California. He also became consultant to the Human Dimensions Foundation, a California-based group investigating new directions in sustainable energy and materials. Many of Muennig's projects have involved innovatory use of solar energy. His work has been published and exhibited throughout the world.
www.bigsuronline.com

Shoei YOH

Shoei Yoh studied at the Keio Gijuku University, Tokyo, graduating in 1962. In 1992 he was appointed Visiting Professor of Architecture at the Graduate School of Architecture, Planning and Preservation, Columbia University, New York. In 1996 he became Professor of Architecture and Urban Design at the Graduate School of Keio University. Awards include the Mainichi Design Award (1983); Japan Institute of Architects Award (1983); Architectural Institute of Japan Award (1989); IAKS Gold Medal (1993); Benedictus Award finalist (1994). In 1997 he published *12 Calisthenics for Architecture* and *In Response to Natural Phenomena*.
www.toto.co.jp
www.taiyokogyo.co.jp

Imre MAKOVECZ

Born in 1935 in Budapest, Imre Makovecz studied architechture at the Technical University of Budapest, graduating in 1959. He worked as architect/designer in the Bureau of Urban Studies, Budapest (1959–62); in Szövterv, Budapest (1962–71); Chief of the Architectural Studio, Vatti, Budapest (1971–77); and was architect/designer to the forestry company Bilis, Budapest (1977–83). In 1983 he established the Mazkona architectural cooperative. He is a member of the board of the Hungarian Architects Association and was awarded the Ybl Prize in 1969.
www.makovecz.hu

John WATSON

Born in 1929 in Austin, Texas; 1954–57 Active member of the Taliesin Fellowship; 1957–59 Associate in the office of Aaron Green, West Coast office of Frank Lloyd Wright, San Francisco; 1960 Wilson residence, first steel and gunite structure; 1963 Stephens' Residence, Austin, Texas; 1965 Artists' Studio Complex, Colony Catherine, Palo Duro Canyon, Texas; 1966–81 Bar P Cross Farm, Devers, Texas; 1968 Personal Residence, Austin; 1972 Goeth Residence, Austin; 1974 McCormick residence, Austin; 1975 Spiller Drive Tri-Plex, Austin; 1980 Lewis Residence "Grotto House", Austin; 1981 Hunt Residence "Nautilus", Lakeway; 1994 Scanlan Compound (pumiscrete), Santa Fe, New Mexico; 1998 McCall Residence, guest house and pool, Pedernales River, Texas; 2000 Keen Residence "Spiral Generation", St. Thomas, Virgin Islands
www.biostructures.net

Steven JOHNSON

Born in Minneapolis, Minnesota, USA, in 1958. he studied architecture at Kansas State University. He later attended the Architectural Association in London between 1987 and 1988 for post diploma studies. Johnson has worked with several London firms including Gus Alexander, Lifschutz Davidson, and Edward Cullinan Architects where he is currently a consultant. His own company The Architecture Ensemble was established in 2000 with the aim of exploiting the virtues of timber through design and building.
e-mail: cullinan@cullinan.demon.co.uk

KOVAL

In his own words:
1958 Born St Bonface, Manitoba, Canada.
1964 Commenced socially demanded attendance at statistically complied mind structuring facility.
1976 Completion of same and entry into socially sanctioned labor force avoidance/status enhancement facility. Bachelor of Environmental Studies, University of Manitoba, Bachelor of Architecture, University of Detroit.
1978–1984 Apprenticeship with European artists in various disciplines on eccclesiastical and monumental works.
1984 Exit academia, entry into Babylon. Five years architectural mercenary.
1989 to present Commissioned work in mediums of architecture, interiors, drawing, leaded glass, monumental, mosaic.
www.thedrive.net/koval

Keith STRUTHERS

Born in 1958 in Johannesburg, South Africa, Struthers worked in farming, freelance illustrating, art festival organizing before designing and constructing crafted buildings for seven years. He then travelled to Europe in 1987 to work and study wetland sewerage systems, clay technology and ecological/organic design. Having completed a post-graduate certificate (IAA) in Russia, he returned to South Africa in December 1991 to open an architectural practice, Natural Architecture. He has also started "Natural Creations", a partnership mass-producing different shaped windows.
www.naturalcreations.co.za

Eugene TSUI

Dr. Eugene Tsui is President of Tsui Design and Research, Inc. with offices in the USA and mainland China. He has studied the profound, interdisciplinary workings of nature as a basis for human-made architecture. Tsui coined the term evolutionary architecture, which refers to the development of new structures, construction materials and processes, ecological relationships, and aesthetic concepts based upon the five-billion-year-old evolutionary development of nature, and has applied these nature-based lessons to human-made environments. His most recent book is *Evolutionary*

Architecture: Nature As A Basis For Design. Tsui's work has been featured in television programmes and film documentaries worldwide.
www.TDRInc.com

Nicholas GRIMSHAW

After studying architecture at the Edinburgh College of Art and the Architectural Association in London, Grimshaw set up his own practice in 1965. Grimshaw has designed several landmark industrial buildings and the practice has won over 70 awards for architecture. Nicholas Grimshaw was awarded the CBE in 1993.

Javier SENOSIAIN

Born in Mexico in 1948, Senosiain graduated in 1972 from the National Independent University of Mexico. Since that time he has combined teaching architecture with practising architecture. His architectural projects have included offices, homes, and industrial and tourist developments. His book *Bioarquitectura, en busca de un espacio* (Bioarchitecture, in Search of a Space) was published in 1996. He is currently involved in an organic residential project, which uses ferrocement on a greater scale than it has been used before.
www.globalnot.com.mx/bioarquitectura/english.htm

Kendrick Bangs KELLOGG

Kellogg attended the University of San Diego State, the University of Colorado, the University of Southern California, and the University of California at Berkeley. He received his architect's license in 1964, since when he has been building organic projects worldwide. He is not only a creative organic builder but also a community planner who was responsible for instituting, in San Diego, the only Planned District Ordinance in the world which allows for compatible neighbourhood character without inhibiting the diversity of any architectural style. He has created the Institute of Organic Architecture in southern California, to provide a centre for learning how to design and build original architecture.
www.sandiegoart.com/KKellogg

Arthur DYSON

Arthur Dyson began his architectural practice in Los Gatos, California in 1963 and in Fresno, California in 1969, where he has practised ever since. He studied psychology at the University of Wisconsin, philosophy at the University of Oklahoma, urban and regional planning at California State University, Fresno, and received a Master of Architecture degree at the San Francisco Institute of Architecture. Dyson is the recipient of over 100 design awards, including the Firm of the Millennium Award from the American Institute of Architects and the 1993 Gold Medal from the Society of American Registered Architects.
www.arthurdyson.com

Useful addresses

Arcosanti
HC 74, Box 4136
Mayer, AZ 86333, USA
Tel: +1 520 632 7135
e-mail: info@arcosanti.org
Website: www.arcosanti.org
(Paolo Soleri's pioneering "arcology"
desert community)

Art Institute of Chicago
111 South Michigan Avenue
Chicago, IL 60603-6110, USA
Website: www.artic.edu
(Bruce Goff Archives)

Bruce Goff Chair of Creative Architecture
University of Oklahoma
830 Van Vleet Oval
Norman, OK 73019, USA
Website: www.arch.ou.edu/a/goff/
(Past holders include Bart Prince, Arthur
Dyson, and Douglas Cardinal)

California Institute of Earth Art and
Architecture (Cal-Earth)
10376 Shangri La Avenue
Hesperia, CA 92345, USA
Tel: +1 760 244 0614
Fax: +1 760 244 2201
e-mail: calearth@aol.com
Website: www.calearth.org
(Nader Khalili's earth-building centre)

Centre Cultural Caixa Catalunya
Provença 261–265
08008 Barcelona, Spain
Tel: +34 93 484 59 95
Fax: +34 93 484 58 89
Website: www.caixacat.es/fund_cat.html
(Espai Gaudí exhibition housed in La
Pedrera)

Ecological Design Association (EDA)
British School, Slad Road, Stroud
Gloucestershire GL5 1QW, England
Tel: +44 (0) 1453 765575
Fax: +44 (0) 1453 759211
e-mail: ecological@designassociation.
freeserve.co.uk
Website: www.edaweb.org

(Non-profit eco-design organization
founded by David Pearson. Publishes
EcoDesign magazine)

Ecological Design Institute (EDI)
10 Libertyship Way, Suite 370
Sausalito, CA 94965, USA
Tel: +1 415 332 5806
Fax: +1 415 332 5808
e-mail: ecodesign@aol.com
Website: www.ecodesign.org/edi
(Non-profit eco-design organization
founded by Sim Van der Ryn)

Eden Project
Watering Lane Nursery
Pentewan, St Austell
Cornwall PL26 6BE, England
Tel: +44 (0) 1726 222900
Fax: +44 (0) 1726 222901
Website: www.cornwall-
calling.co.uk/eden
("Biomes" designed by Nicholas Grimshaw)

Frank Lloyd Wright Foundation
Taliesin West, PO Box 4430
Scottsdale, AZ 85261-4430, USA
Tel: +1 602 860 2700
Fax: +1 602 391 4009
e-mail: fllwfdn@franklloydwright.org
Website: www.franklloydwright.org
(Foundation preserving the legacy of
Frank Lloyd Wright and advancing organ-
ic architecture and education)

Friends of Kebyar, Inc. (FOK)
P.O. Box 550904
Atlanta, Georgia 30355, USA
Tel: +1 404 237 8031
Fax: +1 303 399 0131
e-mail: Friends@kebyar.com
Website: www.kebyar.com
(Publishes *Friends of Kebyar Architectural
Journal* and *Kebyar Network Newsletter*)

Fundación César Manrique
Taro de Tahiche 35509, Teguise
Lanzarote, Canary Islands
Tel: +34 928 84 31 38
Fax: +34 928 84 34 63
e-mail: fcmanrique@feuix.net
(Art gallery and exhibition facilities housed
in former home of César Manrique plus
information on Manrique)

Goetheanum Conference Office
Box, CH-4143 Dornach 1, Switzerland
Tel: +41 61 706 44 44
Fax: +41 61 706 44 46
Website: www.art-advising.de
(Rudolf Steiner anthroposophic art and
architecture exhibitions and conferences)

Real Goods Solar Living Center
13771 S. Highway
Hopland, CA 95449, USA
Tel: +1 707 744 2100
Fax: +1 707 744 1342
Website: www.realgoods.com
(Ecological living centre and store
designed by Sim Van der Ryn Architects)

San Francisco Institute of Architecture
(SFIA)
Information Office
Box 749
Orinda, CA 94563, USA
Tel: +1 925 299 1325
Fax: +1 925 299 0181
e-mail: SFIA@aol.com
Website: www.sfia.net
(Architectural institute teaching organic
and ecological design)

The Earth Centre
Denaby Main
Doncaster DN12 4EA, England
Tel: +44 (0) 1709 512000
Fax: +44 (0) 1709 512010
e-mail: info@earthcentre.org.uk
Website: www.earthcentre.org.uk
(Ecological theme park with buildings
designed by various architects including
The Ark by Future Systems)

The Wetland Centre
The Wildfowl & Wetlands Trust (WWT)
Queen Elizabeth's Walk
London SW13 9SF, England
Tel: +44 (0) 20 8409 4400
Fax: +44 (0) 20 8409 4401
e-mail: info@wetlandcentre.org.uk
Website: www.wwt.org.uk
(Wetland area with public exhibition build-
ings designed by David Pearson)

For other useful information, search the
Internet under "Organic Architecture".

Bibliography

Adams, David "Rudolf Steiner's First Goetheanum as an illustration of Organic Functionalism", *Journal of the Society of Architectural Historians,* June 1992.

Baggs, Sydney and Baggs Joan *The Healthy House,* Harper Collins, Sydney, 1996.

Barnes, Michael "Walk on the Wide Side", *RIBA Journal,* London, May 2000.

Blundell Jones, Peter "Hugo Häring", *Architectural Review,* April 1982.

Blundell Jones, Peter "Organic Architecture", *Architects' Journal,* 20 January 1982.

Blundell Jones, Peter "Organic Response", *Architectural Review,* February 1992.

Blundell Jones, Peter "Departure from the Right-Angle", *Architectural Review,* February 1992.

Blundell Jones, Peter *Hans Scharoun,* Phaidon, London, 1995.

Bornstein, Eli "Notes on the Mechanical and the Organic in Art and Nature", *The Structuralist,* 35/36, 1995.

Borsich, Wolfgang *Lanzarote & César Manrique: 7 Buildings,* Lito. A. Romero, S.A., Tenerife, 1992.

Bovill, Carl *Fractal Geometry in Architecture and Design,* Birkhäuser, Boston, 1996.

Branch, Mark Alden "A Breed Apart", *Progressive Architecture,* Vol. 73 No. 6, June 1992.

Buchanan, P. *Renzo Piano Building Workshop. Complete Works,* Phaidon, London, 1993.

Calmenson, Diane Wintroub "Be Happy, Be Gaia: For David Pearson, Design, Life and Spirit are One", *Interior & Sources Magazine,* USA, July/August 1996.

Calmenson, Diane Wintroub "Learning about Ecological Design with Sim Van der Ryn", *Interior and Sources Magazine,* USA, October 1996.

Carandell, Josep M. *Park Güell: Gaudí's Utopia,* Triangle Books, Menorca, 1998.

Coates, Gary J. *Erik Asmussen,*

Architect, Byggförlaget, Stockholm, 1997.

Cook, Jeffrey *The Architecture of Bruce Goff,* Granada, London, 1978.

Cook, Theodore Andrea *The Curves of Life,* 1914, Dover Publications edition, New York, 1978.

Davey, Peter "Gottfried Böhm", *Architectural Review,* June 1981.

Day, Christopher *Building with Heart,* Green Books, Devon, 1990.

Day, Christopher *Places of the Soul,* Thorsons, London, 1993.

De Long, David G. *Bruce Goff: Toward Absolute Architecture,* MIT Press, Cambridge, Massachusetts and London, 1969 and 1988.

Ebert, Wolfgang M. *Wahnsinn Wohnen,* Edition Fricke, Frankfurt am Main, 1987.

Foley, Heide "Eugene Tsui", *Mondo 2000,* Berkeley, California, Issue No 13.

Gaarder, Jostein *Sophie's World,* Phoenix Paperback, Orion Books, London, 1996.

Garnham, Trevor *Oxford Museum, Oxford 1855–60 Deane and Woodward,* Phaidon, London, 1996.

Ghyka, Matila *The Geometry of Art and Life, 1946,* Dover Publications edition, New York, 1977.

Giralt-Miracle, Daniel & Marz *Fernando Espai Gaudí: Guide La Pedrera, Barcelona,* Centre Cultural Caixa Catalunya, 1998.

Gordillo, Fernando *Ruiz César Manrique,* Fundación César Manrique, 1995.

Grabow, Stephen "Organic and Mechanical Form Principles", *The Structuralist,* 35/36, 1995.

Greenhalgh, Paul (ed.) *Art Nouveau 1890–1914,* V&A Publications, London, 2000.

Haeckel, Ernst *Art Forms in Nature: The Prints of Ernst Haeckel,* Prestel Verlag, Munich & New York, 1998 (reproduction of plates in first edition *Kunstformen der Natur,* Leipzig & Vienna, Bibliographisches Institut, 1904)

Hammonds, Mark *The Architecture of Arthur Dyson,* Fresno Art Museum, California, 1993.

Häring, Hugo "Approaches to Form, 1925–6". English translation of "Wege zur Form" in Benton and Sharp (eds.) *Form and Function,* Open University Publications, Milton Keynes, 1975.

Heathcote, Edwin "Imre Makovecz: The Wings of the Soul", *Architectural Monograph No. 47,* Academy Editions, London, 1997.

Hess, Alan *Hyperwest: American Residential Architecture on the Edge,* Whitney Library of Design, New York, 1996.

Hill, Stevanne "The New Wave", *The Sunday Telegraph Magazine,* London, 31 March 1996.

Hoffmann, Donald *Frank Lloyd Wright: Architecture and Nature,* Dover Publications, New York, 1986.

Iannacci, Anthony *Shoei Yoh: In Response to Natural Phenomena,* L'Arca Edizioni, Italy, 1997.

Jacobs, Herbert *Building with Frank Lloyd Wright: An Illustrated Memoir,* Chronicle, San Francisco, 1978.

Jencks, Charles *The Architecture of the Jumping Universe,* Academy Editions, London, revised edition 1997.

Jodidio, Philip *Santiago Calatrava,* Taschen Verlag, Köln, 1998.

Jones, David Lloyd *Architecture and the Environment: Bioclimatic Building Design,* Laurence King Publishing, London, 1998.

Kellogg, Kendrick Bangs. Regular series of articles about his work entitled "Organic Architecture" in the *San Diego Décor & Style Magazine,* 2001 Publishing Co. Inc., California, USA.

Khalili, Nader *Racing Alone,* Burning Gate Press, Los Angeles, 1990.

Khalili, Nader *Ceramic Houses and Earth Architecture, How to build your own,* CalEarth Press, California, reprinted 1999.

"La Nuove Organicita", Special Issue, *Domus* No 780, March 1996.

Lambourne, Lionel *Utopian Craftsmen: The Arts and Crafts Movement from the Cotswolds to Chicago,* Astragal Books, London, 1980.

Lang, Bob "The State of the Art", *Architects' Journal,* 2 July 1998.

Mead, Christopher *Houses by Bart*

Prince: An American Architecture for the Continuous Present, University of New Mexico Press, Albuquerque, 1991.

Meehan, Aidan *Celtic Design: Spiral Patterns*, Thames & Hudson, London, 1993.

Mumford, Mark "Form Follows Nature: The Origins of American Organic Architecture", *Journal of Architectural Education* 42/3, Spring 1989.

Myerson, Jeremy *Makepeace: A Spirit of Adventure in Craft and Design*, Conran Octopus, London, 1995.

Nash, Eric Peter *Frank Lloyd Wright: Force of Nature*, Smithmark, New York, 1996.

"New Science = New Architecture", *Architectural Design Profile* No 129, Academy Group, London, 1997.

"Organic Architecture", *Architectural Design Profile* 106, Academy Group, London, November–December 1993.

"Organic Architecture", Exhibition Catalogue, Iona Stichting, Ilona Botterweg, 1992.

Papanek, Victor *The Green Imperative: Ecology and Ethics in Design and Architecture*, Thames & Hudson, London, 1995.

Pawley, Martin *Future Systems*, ICA, Corner House Publications, London, 1998.

Pearson, David *Earth to Spirit: In Search of Natural Architecture*, Gaia Books, London; Chronicle Books, San Francisco and Harper Collins, Sydney Australia, 1994. Revised edition, 2000.

Pearson, David *The Gaia Natural House Book*, Gaia Books, London, 2000, *The Gaia Natural House Book*, Fireside, Simon & Schuster, New York, and HarperCollins, Sydney, 1998.

Pearson, David *The Natural House Catalog: Everything you need to create an environmentally friendly home*, Fireside, Simon & Schuster, New York, 1996.

Permanyer, Luís and Levick, Melba *A Stroll Through Modernista Barcelona*, Ediciones Polígrafa, Barcelona, 1999.

Prochazka, Amjad Bohumil *Determinants of Islamic Architecture*, Muslim Architecture Research Program, Zurich, 1988.

Ree, Pieter van der *Rudolf Steiner's Building Impulse and Organic Architecture in the 20th Century*, Indigo Uitgevers, The Netherlands, 1999.

Rigan, Otto *From the Earth Up: The Art and Vision of James Hubbell*, McGraw-Hill, 1979.

Robinson, Sidney K. "The Continuous Present of Organic Architecture", *Architectural Design* Vol. 63 No.7/8, 1993.

Royal Institute of Architects, *An Organic Architecture, The Architecture of Democracy: An Address by Frank Lloyd Wright*, London, 1939.

Royal Institute of British Architects, *The American School of Architecture: The Bruce Goff Legacy*, exhibition catalogue, London, 1985.

Ruskin, John *The Seven Lamps of Architecture*, 1880. Dover Publications edition, New York, 1989.

Saliga, Pauline & Wollever, Mary (eds) *The Architecture of Bruce Goff*, Prestel Verlag, Munich & New York/The Art Institute of Chicago, 1995.

Schaeffer, John *A Place in the Sun: The Evolution of the Real Goods Solar Living Center*, Chelsea Green, Vermont, 1997.

Sergeant, John *Frank Lloyd Wright's Usonian Houses: The Case for Organic Architecture*, Whitney Library of Design, Watson-Guptill Publications, New York, 1984.

Soleri, Paolo *Arcology: The City in the Image of Man*, MIT Press, Cambridge, Massachusetts, 1969.

Steele, James *The Complete Architecture of Balkrishna Doshi: Rethinking Modernism for the Developing World*, Thames & Hudson, London, 1998.

Sullivan, Louis H. *Kindergarten Chats and Other Writings*, 1918. Dover Publications edition, New York, 1979.

"Sustainable Architecture: Responsive Hübner, Yeang's Bioclimatic Towers", *Architectural Review*, September 1996.

Swan, James *Dialogues with the Living Earth*, Quest Books, 1996.

Thompson, D'Arcy Wentworth *On Growth and Form*, Cambridge University Press, Cambridge, New York and Melbourne, 1917. Reprinted paperback edition, 1997.

Thorne, Tony "Let's Go Organic", *Hot Air*, Virgin Atlantic's in-flight magazine, October–December 1997.

Tsui, Eugene *Evolutionary Architecture: Nature as a Basis for Design*, John Wiley, New York, 1999.

Tzonis, Alexander and Lefaivre, Liane *Architecture in Europe: Memory and Invention since 1968*, Thames & Hudson, paperback edition 1997.

Ushida Findlay, *Parallel Landscapes*, Toto, Japan, 1996.

Ushida Findlay, *2G International Architecture Review*, No 6, 1998, Editorial Gustavo Gili, Barcelona.

Van der Ryn, Sim with Cowan, Stuart *Ecological Design*, Island Press, Washington DC,1996.

Van Eck, Caroline *Organicism in Nineteenth-Century Architecture: An inquiry into its theoretical and philosophical background*, Architectura & Natura Press, Amsterdam, 1994.

Wilcock, Richard "Organicism", *Archetype*, May 1995.

Zerbst, Rainer *Antoni Gaudí*, Taschen Verlag, Köln, 1993.

Zevi, Bruno "Organic in Italy", *Architectural Review*, June 1985.

Zevi, Bruno *Towards an Organic Architecture*, Faber & Faber, London, 1945.

Index

Acknowledgements

Author's acknowledgements

First and foremost, I would like to give my personal thanks to all the creative organic architects who spared time from their busy schedules to provide their words and pictures for this book and, of course, for their great inspiration. I am indebted to Carol Venolia who gave initial help with introductions in the USA to West Coast organic architects.

My special thanks to all those at Gaia Books who have given help, support and enthusiasm throughout this exciting project. Most of all to Charlie Ryrie for her invaluable assistance in research and obtaining (and, in some cases, skillfully translating) contributions of the many featured architects, Patrick Nugent for his creative and inspired graphic design and, with Pip Morgan, for overall project management. Thanks too to Bridget Morley for her sensitive picture selection and layouts, Cathy Meeus for her calm and professional editorial expertise, Lyn Kirby for production, and Suzy Boston, Frank Chambers and the sales team. And, an especial thanks to my wife Joss for her personal support.

Finally, I would like to acknowledge all those great organic architects of the past from Antoni Gaudí and Rudolf Steiner to Bruce Goff and Frank Lloyd Wright who have laid the foundations of a living organic architecture. Their heritage lives on to inspire us today and for generations to come.

Gaia Books would also like to thank Christian Gotch and Barney Duly for translating the contributions by Peter Hübner and Imre Makovecz respectively and Lynn Bresler for proof-reading the text and compiling the index.

Photographic credits

Photographs by David Pearson unless otherwise stated. While every effort has been made to contact and credit copyright holders, Gaia Books would like to apologise for any errors and omissions.

t = top; b = bottom; r = right; l = left; c = centre; i = inset.

2/3 Szànto Tamàs. 7 Bart Prince/Alan Weintraub. 8 Adrian Senior, Anigraph (dp?). 9 Wetlands Centre/Martin Senior). 14/15 Douglas Cardinal Architects. 16/17 Balkrishna Doshi. 22/23 Renzo Piano/J. Gowna. 24/25 Jacques Gillet. 33 Richard Bryant/Arcaid. 36 Ezra Stoller/Esto /Arcaid. 37 Solomon R. Guggenheim Museum. 38 Hazel Cook/Architectural Association Photo Library. 38/39 T. Street-Porter/Architectural Association Photo Library. 40 Christopher Day. 42 (l) Roderick Coyne; (r) Katsuhisa Kida. 46/47 Nicholas Kane/Arcaid. 50 Andrew Syred/Science Photo Library. 52 (l) John Barlow; (r) Claude Nuridsany & Marie Perennou/Science Photo Library. 54 (l) Future Systems; (r) Eye of Science/ Science Photo Library. 55 (l) D. Cavagnaro; (r) British Architectural Library, RIBA, London. 56 (r) Bart Prince/Alan Weintraub. 57 (l) Szanto Tamas (r) D. Cavagnaro. 58 (l) D. Cavagnaro. 58/59 Bart Prince/Alan Weintraub. 59 (l) D. Cavagnaro; (ir) Ford Motor Company. 60 (t) D. Cavagnaro; (b) N. Grimshaw. 61 (t) D. Cavagnaro; (b) K. Kellogg. 63 Ch. Bastin & J. Evrard. 64 (l) D. Cavagnaro; (r) B&W Products. 66 (b) Bautoro j.o.p.r.l. 68/69 (background and t) Alfred Pasieka/Science Photo Library; (b) Natalie Tepper/Arcaid. 69 (l) Natalie Tepper/ Arcaid; (r, t and b) Daniel Lebiskind. 72/73 Peter Knowles Photography. 74 (t) Russell D. Curtis/Science Photo Library; (b) Eric Kuhne Architects. 78 Douglas Cardinal. 78/79 Jay Mroczek. 79 Steve Teague. 80/81 Archive-Senosiain. 82/83 Aga Khan Trust for Culture/Fabrizio Carola. 84/85 Fabrizio Carola. 86 (t) Bart Prince/Alan Weintraub; (b) Bart Prince. 86/87 Bart Prince. 88/89 Bart Prince/Alan Weintraub.

90/91 Bart Prince. 91 Bart Prince. 92 Bart Prince/Alan Weintraub. 93 Bart Prince. 94–99 Jacques Gillet. 100–103 Erik Asmussen. 104–109 Douglas Cardinal. 107 (t) J.A. Kraulis/ Douglas Cardinal. 108/109 The Postcard Factory. 110–111 Greg Burgess. 112 (t) Trevor Main; (b) Craig Lamotte. 112/113 Greg Burgess. 113 Trevor Main. 114 Sim Van Der Ryn. 114/115 Richard Barnes. 118 Alain Maes. 119 (t) Alain Maes; (b) Eric Furnémont. 121 Eric Furnémont. 122 (t) Jay Mroczek; (b) Daniel Liebermann. 122/123 Jay Mroczek; 123 (inset) Jay Mroczek. 123 Bentley Aerial Photography. 125 (l) Allen Geller; (tr) Jay Mroczek; (br) Daniel Liebermann. 126 Jay Mroczek. 127 Daniel Liebermann. 128 (t) Daniel Liebermann; (b) Jay Mroczek. 129 Jay Mroczek. 130–133 Balkrishna Doshi. 134–135 Yatin Pandya. 136 Shigeo Ogawa. 137 (t) Tadao Ando Architect & Associates (inset) Shigeo Ogawa; (b) Mitsuo Matsuoka. 138/139 Hubbell Studio/Jerry Rife. 140–141 Chuck Kimbell. 142–143 Vitor Ruivo Forte. 144/147 Renzo Piano/John Gollings. 148 Katsuhisha Kida. 149 Ushida Findlay Partnership. 151 (tl,bl) Katsuhisha Kida; (tr) Ushida Findlay Partnership; (br) Katsuhisha Kida. 152–157 Mickey Muennig. 158–161 Peter Hübner. 162 –165 Shoei Yoh & Architects. 166–171 Imre Makovecz/Szànto Tamàs. 172–175 John Watson. 176–177 Steven Johnson. 178–179 Koval. 180–181 Keith Struthers. 182–185 Eugene Tsui. 186–187 Nicolas Grimshaw & Partners; 188 (l) Simon Doling; (r) Nicholas Grimshaw & Partners. 189 Apex Photo Agency. 190 Archive-Senosiain. 190/191 Jaime Jacott. 191–195 Archive-Senosiain. 196–199 Kendrick Bangs Kellogg. 200/201 Dr. S.Yen. 201 Kendrick Bangs Kellogg. 202–205 Rau & Partners. 206/207 Arthur Dyson. 208 Zimmerman. 208/209, 209 Arthur Dyson. 210 (t) Samyn & Associates; (b) Daylight Liège sprl. 210/211 Ch. Bastin & J.Evrard. 211 Ch. Bastin & J.Evrard. 212–213 Matteo Piazza.